QUICK PREP

Founding a Startup
What You Need to Know

Terri Krivosha

For additional copies or customer service inquiries, please e-mail west.customer.service@thomson.com.

ISBN 978-0-314-29267-4

Mat #41686460

ACKNOWLEDGMENT

I want to thank Thomson Reuters, Isabel Kunkle, and Ryann Burnett for reaching out to me to discuss the initial idea for this book. Ryann was a great editor and I appreciate her insight and assistance.

The genesis of this book was a class I teach at the William Mitchell College of Law in St. Paul, Minnesota, called "The Startup Business Enterprise." I want to thank the College, Thuy Vo, who had the original idea for the class and has been a wonderful mentor to me, and Louis Ainsworth, the current executive director of the William Mitchell "Business and Law Center" for his insight on my course. I want to thank my students in "The Startup Business Enterprise." As it says in the Talmud, I have learned much from my teachers, even more from my colleagues, but I have learned the most from my students. They have truly been and continue to be an inspiration to me.

My associate at Maslon Edelman Borman & Brand LLP, Kathleen Crowe, took my class in the fall of 2013 and helped me tremendously by drafting the initial "takeaways" from each chapter. My partners at the Maslon Law Firm have supported and encouraged me in all my endeavors and I thank them for their friendship, support, and guidance for the past twenty-one years.

Finally, saving the best for last, I want to thank my family. I learned from my parents, Norman and Helene Krivosha, the meaning of confidence. I learned from my son, Avi, and my daughter-in-law, Shaina, the meaning of humility. From my daughter, Tamar, I learned courage, tenacity, and the unending capacity for strength. My husband, Hayim, has been my soul mate, my best friend, and my biggest fan for thirty-eight years. Without his encouragement and wise counsel this book, and my career in general, would not have been possible.

DEDICATION

To Hayim, my soul mate.

CONTENTS

1

What Is a Successful Business?

"It had long since come to my attention that people of accomplishment rarely sat back and let things happen to them, they went out and happened to things." - Leonardo De Vinci

I teach a class called the "Startup Business Enterprise" at the William Mitchell School of Law in St. Paul, Minnesota. The class is part of the school's Business and Law Center and is taught more like a course in business school rather than a course in law school. The first year I taught, a law professor signed up to audit the course. He had an idea for a business and thought he would benefit from participating. We met prior to the first class to discuss his business idea. He came with lists of documents he would need and which of his research assistants would prepare each of the documents. I let him talk for most of the lunch about his idea and show me his lists. When he finished, I asked one simple question: Where is the page with your business plan, your projections, and your funding requirements? There was not one number in any of the pages he had shown me. He grinned a bit sheepishly and said, "I thought you were going to say that."

Development of a business is a process that does not happen overnight, but often is a result of one's prior experiences both at work and in private life. During the thirty-one years that I have practiced law, I have observed startup businesses that were successful and others that were not. Through the years, I have focused on identifying what I believe are the elements, that when present, make it more likely than not that a startup will be successful. I will share those with you throughout the pages of this book.

But before I provide my thoughts, let us first consider what others, who have different experiences than me, have said about creating a successful business.

The Best Leaders

Jim Collins begins his most recent book, *Great by Choice*,[1] by advising the reader, "We cannot predict the future. But we can create it." Collins' book answered the question, "Why do some companies thrive in uncertainty, even chaos, and others do not?" What he and his research team found surprised those who are students of business success. They found:

- *The best leaders were not more risk taking, more visionary, and more creative than the comparisons; they were more disciplined, more empirical, and more paranoid.*
- *Innovation by itself turns out not to be the trump card in a chaotic and uncertain world; more important is the ability to scale innovation, to blend creativity with discipline.*
- *Following the belief that leading in a "fast world" always requires "fast decisions" and "fast action" is a good way to get killed.*
- *The great companies changed less in reaction to a radically changing world than the comparison companies.*

Collins identifies the characteristics of successful companies as fanatic discipline, productive paranoia, and empirical creativity. He posits that while business leaders cannot always control the world around them, how they react to those forces is what distinguishes a successful company from an unsuccessful one.

For Collins, "fanatic discipline" is the "independence of mind to reject pressures to conform in ways incompatible with values, performance standards, and long-term aspirations." I would call this concept the need to never let go of your "moral compass." The moral compass each of us brings to our own business will inform what we do and how we act. If we ignore the pull of our moral compass and instead succumb to pressure to follow a different direction, we risk losing sight of those attributes that will help to define the success of a startup business.

---

[1] JIM COLLINS & MORTEN T. HANSEN, GREAT BY CHOICE (2011).

"Productive paranoia" according to Collins is "hypervigilence in good times as well as bad—consistently consider the possibility that events can turn against you without warning." I would call this, never taking your "eye off the ball." I have seen companies during my career become "fat and happy" in good times, only to decline when times are worse. For a business to be successful, its leadership must always be thinking proactively about what the future might bring. When times are good, it is more important for leadership to be focused, because they have the time and luxury to plan. When planning is required because an emergency is imminent, leadership has less control over the outcome.

Finally, Collins' third core behavior is "empirical creativity," which he defines as "relying on direct observation, conducting practical experiments and/or engaging directly with evidence rather than relying upon opinion, whim, conventional wisdom, authority or untested ideas." Collins is a social scientist and so we expect he would suggest that evidence is critical to making sound business decisions. But even for those of us who are not social scientists, Collins provides good advice. I have seen companies time and again think they know what their customers want. Often, I have asked the leadership of these companies whether they have done focus groups and actually consulted with customers to find out if the way the company wants to deliver products and services is the way its customers want to receive them. More times than I can count, they have been very silent before answering this question, realizing that they have not consulted their customers and simply assumed an answer. For a business to satisfy the needs of its customers and to continually improve the products or services provided, *leadership must truly understand the scope of its customers' needs.*

Collins couples these core behaviors with something he calls "level 5 ambition." By this he means individuals "who channel their ego and intensity into something more enduring than themselves." My experience has taught me that a leader who can channel his or her egotism into developing a company that is bigger than any one individual will be successful. Those entrepreneurs who think building a company is all about themselves seldom, if ever, succeed.

I would recommend that those who are starting companies use these "core behaviors" as well as level 5 ambition, as coined by Collins, as a benchmark to help keep them focused as they begin to put together their business plans. It is important every so often to step back, make sure the leadership team has not lost focus, and readjust if necessary.

Make Meaning

Although these core behaviors as identified by Collins are an important ballast in the sea of the "startup business," I believe that Guy Kawasaki's advice in *The Art of the Start*[2] is just as important. Kawasaki begins the first chapter of his book with the following Hasidic saying: "Everyone should carefully observe which way his heart draws him, and then choose that way with all his strength." Embodied within this saying is Kawasaki's advice to do the following:

1. Make meaning
2. Make mantra
3. Get going
4. Define your business model
5. Weave a mat (milestones, assumptions, and tasks)

Kawasaki advises an entrepreneur to decide whether or not he or she "wants to make meaning," before embarking on the development of a company. "Meaning" according to Kawasaki does not include wealth, power or prestige. Rather he would ascribe the following to the meaning of "meaning":

- *Make the world a better place*
- *Increase the quality of life*
- *Right a terrible wrong*
- *Prevent the end of something good*

What Kawasaki calls "meaning," I would call passion. Many years ago when I had just been elected chair of my law firm, I attended a seminar for new law firm leaders. One of the speakers explained that she had left her very successful position in a private equity firm because she had lost her passion. At that time, I did not quite understand what "passion" had

---

[2] GUY KAWASAKI, THE ART OF THE START (2004).

to do with success. Several years later, however, the correlation between passion and success is clear to me. Unless an entrepreneur has passion for the problem he or she hopes to solve, his or her business will not be successful. It is the passion that drives each of us to bound out of bed in the morning excited to take on the challenges of the day. If you do not feel this way about what your company is going to do, think long and hard about whether you want to embark on such an endeavor.

Second, Kawasaki would ask you to "create a mantra." This expression is his shorthand for identifying the kind of "meaning" your organization will make. Rather than writing a mission statement, Kawasaki advises to "postpone writing your mission statement…instead of a mission statement, and all the baggage that comes with it, craft a mantra for your organization." He quotes the definition of mantra as: "A sacred verbal formula repeated in prayer, meditation, or incantation, such as an invocation of a god, a magic spell, or a syllable or portion of scripture containing mystical potentialities." Read this definition of mantra again. According to Kawasaki, "A mantra should contain the essence of the meaning you want to make in your company." Try to capture this concept in no more than three or four words. It should easily convey to you and your employees and team the change you want to make in the world. A "mantra" may never have external visibility, but it is an easy to memorize shorthand of your company's attempt to "make meaning."

Finally, Kawasaki advises to use the following principles to "get going."

- *Think big*
- *Find a few soul mates*
- *Polarize people*
- *Use prototypes as market research*

Let us examine each of these suggestions in more depth. For Kawasaki, "thinking big" requires an entrepreneur and his team to set their "sights high and strive for something grand." Funders, when first reviewing a company's business plan, will look both for passion and the unmet need that the company will fill which will change the world. I would advise you to be bold in this initial stage.

Kawasaki believes, and I agree, that successful companies are not begun by sole entrepreneurs. Successful companies depend on a team that has complementary skills, challenges each other, and has collective and individual passion and commitment to the idea at hand.

Kawasaki's advice to "polarize people" means that unless the product or service you create is loved by some and hated by others, it will not be successful. Potential customers cannot feel "neutral" about your product for it to succeed. They must either be early adopters, in which case you should be interviewing them to determine what it is they like about your product or service and what they think you might be able to improve, or they will be naysayers, and these people too are a good source of research. Ask them questions as to why they think your product or service will not work.

My experience with entrepreneurs who have not been successful is that they are perfectionists to the point where they cannot release a product unless they are confident it is the best iteration possible. On the other hand, entrepreneurs with successful businesses release products or services more quickly and learn from customers regarding how to make their products or services better. Perfectionism should be anathema to an entrepreneur. Successful companies work with their teams to constantly upgrade their products or services while at the same time finding early adopters to purchase them.

I am an early adopter. I purchased a treadmill desk from Steele Case in 2009 when they were first being sold commercially. I received a three-year warranty because I was an early adopter, burned through three motors, which likely needed to be improved, and provided advice on how to make the product better. I am thrilled that I purchased the product four years ago rather than waiting until it was perfect. Since I purchased a treadmill desk, I have walked two miles a day, lost weight, and felt better. I would not have wanted to wait until the desk had been perfected. So, my advice to entrepreneurs is to find early adopters and reward them.

Timing to market is also a critical element in the success of a startup. It is important to consider early in the life of your business who your competitors are. Determine how fast you need to roll out your first product or service to be successful, and try your hardest to adhere to your timeline.

Reasons Entrepreneurs Start Businesses

Why do entrepreneurs tend to start businesses? I have seen several reasons over the years.

Because an entrepreneur:

- Cannot work for anyone else
- Has a good idea
- Wants to develop a product he or she himself or herself wants to use
- Has had one or more successes and has developed a team in which others will invest

The Real World

Julie Gilbert Newrai is a serial entrepreneur who took Kawasaki's words to heart. After developing seven businesses inside Deloitte and Best Buy, including Virgin Mobile joint venture, Magnolia Home Theatre, WOLF innovation platform (which enabled her to work directly with Nintendo engineers to create Nintendo wii), Motorola (creation of MOTOACTV wearable fitness devices), and many others, she left her post as Best Buy's senior vice president of enterprise growth and innovation to build her own consulting firm. She later married and had a baby. Eight weeks after her son was born, her husband had a major stroke and brain surgery, spent a month in intensive care and then transitioned to a rehabilitation center. After Julie went back to work, she was constantly worried about her son and her husband. One day, she decided to check in by calling both her husband's rehabilitation center and her son's daycare. After two calls to each place were dropped, she pulled over to the side of the road and in her words had a short "pity party." Then she decided something needed to be done to enable people to get information about the people they love. She will tell you she is a little bit stubborn—a very important characteristic of an entrepreneur. She decided that day to create PreciouStatus, a technology platform that enables professional caregivers to give real-time updates to subscribers.

Julie believes that to develop a successful business you need to start with partnerships where everyone wins. You need passion and patience. Assume it will take three times as much money and twice as long. In addition to building relationships and networking, for a business to be successful you must innovate and give back. Determine the problem that exists and develop a business model that will alleviate the pain caused by the problem.

Although Julie knew nothing about childcare centers or rehab centers when she started PreciouStatus, she knew there was a need and is developing a business to meet that need.

Takeaways from Chapter 1

- *First*, follow your moral compass.
- *Second*, keep your eye on the ball.
- *Third*, do your homework.
- *Fourth*, maintain passion, not perfectionism.
- *Fifth*, strive for everyone to win and maintain balance.

2

Business Planning

"Plans are useless, but planning is everything."
- Dwight D. Eisenhower

Reflecting on elaborate, heavily detailed business plans as well as simple "back of the napkin" business plans, I would advise entrepreneurs beginning a startup business to create a plan with a level of detail in between those two extremes.

Importance of Writing a Business Plan

Writing a business plan for a startup business is important for several reasons. The process itself will help the founders identify the focus of their endeavor. Often, an entrepreneur's original idea will change when he or she puts pen to paper to develop a plan for the business. In addition, the business planning process helps the business leaders develop their pitch for investors and customers (See Chapter 8). A road map is a useful analogy for a business plan, and detours, dead ends, and faulty directions are obstacles to expect. So you are advised to keep your "paper map" for a bit as your ideas germinate and develop.

Guy Kawasaki tells you "to write the plan as if it is deliberate but be prepared to act as if it is emergent." In other words, a business plan must be fluid and susceptible to change.

Why Do Research

A business plan should not be solely developed out of "thin air" and the ideas of the founders. There needs to be some degree of research as part of the initial phase. The next part of this chapter will give you some ideas as to how to begin the business planning process.

Often, entrepreneurs think that they need to determine who the direct competition is, and based on that research, develop a plan. However, Michael E. Porter developed an analysis now called "Porter's Five Forces,"[3] which helps to analyze the strategies and weaknesses of a business. Porter's five competitive forces are not something you would insert into a business plan, but his process of analysis is a research guide to better understand who your direct competitors are and keep in mind the five forces Porter believes will shape your company's competition in its industry.

Porter's Five Forces are:

- *Rivalry among existing competitors*
- *Threat of new entrants*
- *Bargaining power of buyers*
- *Threat of substitute products or services*
- *Bargaining power of suppliers*

---
[3] See generally Michael E. Porter, *How Competitive Forces Shape Strategy*, HARV. BUS. REV., Mar.-Apr. 1979.

Let us look at each of the Five Forces in a bit more depth:

Competitive Rivalry: This is competition that already exists. It is likely that as a founder you are aware of at least some of the companies you view as your competitors. Part of the challenge of defining your business is to identify how your business will set you apart. For example, if your business is a commodity and there are many competitors in the market, you will have to compete on price. If your business has fewer competitors, you can compete on quality. You need to compare what you can offer and what your competitors can offer which will help to give you an understanding of the environment in which your company will live.

Threat of New Entrants: Consider how hard it will be to break into the new business that is the focus of your startup. Is there a low barrier to entry or high barrier to entry? For example, if your business is a day care center, the barrier to entry is low because there are numerous day cares and the resources and skills needed to establish one are not difficult to attain compared to other industries. However, if your business is a diamond mine your barrier to entry is high because the resources and skills needed to begin require a high degree of education and the location of appropriate natural resources.

Substitute Products or Services: Consider other companies who provide a product or service that is similar to the product or service your company will provide. These are the companies against whom you will be competing. For example, if you lived in New York City and had to travel to Washington, DC, a new airline has to look not only at competing airlines but should think about buses and trains as competitors. McDonald's cannot only look at Burger King and Wendy's as competitors but Chipotle, Noodles, and other similar fast food restaurants.

Bargaining Power of Buyers: This factor relates to supply and demand. Consider how many customers need or want what your company will offer. How easy will it be for a customer to get what your company will offer from some other business? For example, a company that is a monopoly like a cable company will have greater bargaining power than a company that sells candy bars.

Bargaining Power of Suppliers: When examining this factor, you should analyze what the competitive threat is of new entrants into the industry from which you will purchase your supplies. The higher the bargaining power of suppliers, the lower the margins of your new company. For example, if you are manufacturing clothing and the price of cotton rises, you can likely find another supplier. If, on the other hand, you need a constant supply of gasoline (because, for example, you have trucks that deliver your product or service), it will likely be difficult to find another supplier.

How necessary is it for a startup to have a business plan? It is important as a guide but never let the plan become an end unto itself. Use it instead as a means to maintain focus on your business.

Babson College did a study where it analyzed 116 businesses started by its alumni who graduated between 1985 and 2003.[4] The study compared success measures such as annual revenue, employee numbers, and net income. It found that there was no statistical difference in success between those businesses that started with *formal written plans* than those without them. However, the study did not track the sort of planning these companies did aside from "formal business plans." The analysis, planning, teamwork, and vision used in drafting a plan are useful—just do not get so involved in the process you forget to start your business!

One of the elements that the Porter analysis will help you determine is the extent to which you need to distinguish the product or service your company will offer. It is critical to position your service or product so that potential customers will see its value and its uniqueness.

Research Tips

Before you begin to develop your business plan, however, there is some basic research that you will need to do. The rest of this chapter is a roadmap to jumpstart your research process.

Market Analysis: To do a proper market analysis, you need to understand the segments your company will attract. For example, if your startup was a

---

[4] JULIAN E. LANGE ET AL., PRE-STARTUP FORMAL BUSINESS PLANS AND POST-STARTUP PERFORMANCE: A STUDY OF 116 NEW VENTURES (2007).

movie theatre, the various considerations and segments are the following: your customer base will be those individuals who watch the movie, they will also buy tickets, need a place to park and want to watch the movie while eating snacks they purchase in your theater. To begin your analysis, divide your market into different segments. In our movie theatre example the different segments could be children, parents, tech-savvy consumers, those with cars, those who take public transportation, and those who want a combined dining/movie experience. You *do not* want to concentrate on all of these segments. This exercise is simply to identify *all* the segments so that you can determine on which segments your business will focus. As you begin a company, I suggest that "less is more." Trying to create a company with too broad a brush will not be to your best advantage. Focus, focus, focus, and focus on the segments you want to serve. You will need to figure out how to access the segments on which you want to concentrate and the unique attributes of the segments and the latest trends in the market that will help you succeed.

To conduct a market analysis for the initial stages of writing a business plan, you need to make sure that the products or services you want to offer will appeal to the customers you want to serve. Consider the answers to the three following questions as you begin your journey:

- *Who, if anyone, has a real need for the thing I propose to sell, and how many of those potential customers are there?*
- *How much, if anything, are those potential customers spending to address that need today?*
- *Does my product or service meet that need in a manner that either saves the customer money or makes them money?*

It is relatively easy today to do some online focus groups with your target market. There are several Internet tools (e.g., Survey Monkey[5]) that will allow you to create surveys to further understand the segments you want to address. The questions must be carefully crafted to elicit the information you want. Also, today there are many online forums that might be centered on your business segment where you could post questions and do research.

---

[5] SURVEYMONKEY, https://www.surveymonkey.com/.

Use the Internet to look for businesses in the segment where you want to start a business to see how you can get "smart" from them.

Consult Susan Gunelius' article in ENTREPRENEUR[6] for a list of affordable consumer research tools. Also, consult Jean Scheid's article on BRIGHT HUB PM[7] for help on conducting market analysis for a business plan.

The Real World

According to Dan Mallin, serial successful entrepreneur and currently the managing partner of Magnet 360, a business plan helps you understand how to tell your story and is a document you live by, modify, and understand. Oftentimes business plans are used at the beginning of a venture to sell a product or raise funds, then shelved and only taken out when there is a problem. Dan would advise that the business plan become a living document that founders are constantly reviewing and changing.

A potential investor always has the option to stop reading a business plan. Therefore, it is essential that the plan catch the reader's attention immediately. It is important to identify your segment of the market that you intend to capture; the narrower your focus, the more likely your ideas will have traction with potential customers and investors. Do as much research as possible to learn about your segment.

Dan also advises entrepreneurs to be nimble and adapt to changes in their businesses. Listen to what others say about what they believe works and does not work in your business plan. Above all, learn to tell your story, quickly, with passion and succinctly.

Takeaways from Chapter 2

- *First*, engage in the process of business planning, in moderation.
- *Second*, hone in on the reasons why your business is unique.
- *Third*, determine the optimal segment of the market to target.

---

[6] Susan Gunelius, *Five Affordable Consumer Research Tools*, ENTREPRENEUR (Dec. 11, 2011), www.entrepreneur.com/article/222389.
[7] Jean Scheid, *The Agile Triangle: More than Scope, Schedule and Cost*, BRIGHT HUB PM, www.brighthub.com/office/entrepreneurs/articles/50212.aspx (last updated Jan. 8, 2014).

- *Fourth*, position the business so that potential customers appreciate its value.
- *Fifth*, be mindful of changes in your business and industry, and adapt quickly.

3

The Zen of Financial Statements and Financial Projections

"Chance favors the mind that is prepared." - Louis Pasteur

Do not stop reading or breathing yet. If you are like the professor I mentioned in Chapter 1 and do not know too much about financial statements, let alone projections, this chapter will help you to develop the basic skills you need. If you believe you are well versed in financial statements, you may want to skip to the section on financial projections or simply move on. I find, however, that no matter how many years I have reviewed financial statements and projections, I learn something each time I review the basic terms and reasons for the various statements.

Financial statements and projections need to tell a story. The challenge of an entrepreneur is to enable others to hear your story while reviewing your numbers.

Financial Statements

Financial statements have three basic components—a balance sheet, an income statement, and a cash flow statement. These statements together present the financial condition of the company for a certain period.

The balance sheet is a "snapshot" of your company at a certain date. For that reason the balance sheet indicates its information is "at" the last date of the period for which the financial statements provide information.

The balance sheet identifies (1) what the company owns—these are its "assets," (2) claims others have against the company—these are its liabilities, and (3) the equity the owners have in the business.

When you look at a balance sheet the assets will always be on the left side of the statement and should be in a standard order from most liquid asset (i.e., cash) to least liquid asset (i.e., goodwill). Liabilities are always on the right side of the balance sheet and are listed first by those that are most current (i.e., due within one year) to those that are long term (due over more than one year). The liabilities of long-term debt that must be paid within one year are listed in the current liabilities and subtracted from the listing of long-term liabilities.

A balance sheet must "balance." The amount of assets on the balance sheet must be equal to the amount of liabilities PLUS the owners' equity, or to put it another way, Assets - Liabilities = Owners' Equity. For example, if your total assets are $500,000 and your total liabilities are $50,000 then your owners' equity is equal to $500,000-$50,000= $450,000. An example of a balance sheet using the accrual method of accounting is the following:

BALANCE SHEET AT END OF FIRST YEAR OF BUSINESS[8]

Start-Up Co.

Current Assets			Current Liabilities		
Cash		$243,000	Accounts Payable		$269,120
Accounts Receivable		405,000	Accrued Expenses		130,390
Inventory		632,400	Income Tax Payable		10,200
Prepaid Expenses		77,760	Short-Term Notes Payable		300,000
Total Current Assets		$1,358,160	Total Current Liabilities		$709,710
			Long-Term Notes Payable		525,000
Property, Plant & Equipment			Stockholders' Equity		
Land, Building, Machines,	918,000		Capital Stock	$766,030	
Equipment and Furniture			Retained Earnings	198,000	
Accumulated Depreciation	(78,200)	840,580			964,030
Total Assets		$2,198,740	Total Liabilities & Stockholders' Equity		$2,198,740

The income statement is sometimes referred to as a "profit and loss statement," "P&L," an "earnings statement," an "operating statement," or a "statement of operations." Do not let the nomenclature fool you. The point

---

[8] JOHN A. TRACY, HOW TO READ A FINANCIAL REPORT 10 (3d ed., 1989).

of the income statement is to summarize a company's sales, net profit, expenses, and net income over a period of time. For that reason, an income statement always indicates it is for the _____ month period *ending* on a certain date. Reviewing an income statement provides a great deal of information regarding the amount of revenue the company receives for sales of goods or services, the amount of money that is required to produce the product or service and operate the company, and the amount remaining after accounting for all expenses.

The format of the income statement always starts with the gross sales number. A company will subtract from gross sales the cost to produce the product or service it sells. This cost may be referred to as "COGS" (i.e., cost of goods sold). Certain expenses directly related to the manufacture of a product or the rendering of a service are deducted from the gross sales number to arrive at the company's "net profit." From the net profit number, a company deducts the operating expenses needed to run the company. The number on an income statement after the operating expenses are deducted is often referred to as EBIT (i.e., "Earnings Before Interest and Taxes"). Sometimes this number may be broadened and referred to as EBITDA. This means "Earnings Before Interest, Taxes, Depreciation and Amortization." Each owner of a company will determine his or her appetite for debt, how he or she will depreciate a company's assets and pay its debt. Therefore, what often matters most to an investor or potential buyer of a company is the company's EBIT or EBITDA.

An example of an income statement is the following:

INCOME STATEMENT FOR FIRST YEAR[9]

Sales Revenue		$4,212,000
Cost of Goods Sold Expense		2,740,400
Gross Margin		$1,471,600
Operating Expenses	$1,010,880	
Depreciation Expense	78,220	1,089,100
Operating Expense		$ 382,500
Interest Expense		82,500
Earnings Before Income Tax		$ 300,000
Income Tax Expense		102,000
Net Income		$ 198,000

---

[9] *Id.* at 11.

Remember that an income statement shows the company's sales, profit, and operating expenses. It does not have anything to do with cash.

The third financial statement, however, does have everything to do with cash. It is called the Cash Flow Statement. It shows the inflows and outflows to a company during a specific period of time. From a cash flow statement you should be able to identify the cash at the beginning of the period, the receipts by the company for various things (e.g., sales, sale of assets, customers deposits, customer loans), and the cash at the end of the period. The cash flow statement will also identify how the funds that were taken in by the company were used. Typically, these sorts of things include salaries, other operating expenses, loan payments, capital expenditures, and tax payments (unless the structure of the entity is such that it does not pay taxes). From a cash flow statement you should be able to identify how much cash is needed by the company for the period in question and identify if the cash coming into the company is sufficient to cover the outflows. The amount of cash needed to cover the required outflows is often called the "nut" or the "burn rate." If the "nut" or "burn rate" is higher than the amount of cash coming in, a company must determine how to bridge the gap, through investor dollars or loans or by decreasing the dollars needed to run the company. An example of a cash flow statement is:

SUMMARY OF CASH RECEIPTS AND DISBURSEMENT DURING FIRST YEAR[10]

Cash Receipts

From customers for products sold to them	$3,807,000	
From stockholders for which stock shares were issued	766,030	
From borrowing on interest-bearing notes payable	825,000	
Total cash receipts during year		$5,398,030

Cash Disbursements

For purchase of products that were sold or are being held for sale	$3,162,000	
For many different expenses of operating the business	913,680	
For interest on notes payable	68,750	
For income tax based on taxable income of year	91,800	

---

[10] *Id.* at 3.

For land, building, machinery, equipment and furniture purchased at start of year, which will last several years	918,800	
Total cash disbursements during year		5,155,030

Increase in Cash during year, which is balance of Cash at end of year	$243,000

The cash flow statement also helps a company to see trends and develop its milestones—i.e., those target points where decisions will be made. Examples of milestones are achievement of a certain amount of committed revenue from customers, or receipt of an approval needed by a certain time. By identifying these milestones, a company can identify the amount of money it may need from investors to accomplish its goals over a specific period of time.

Summary

The chart below shows the connections among the balance sheet, income statement, and cash flows.

MASTER EXHIBIT[11]

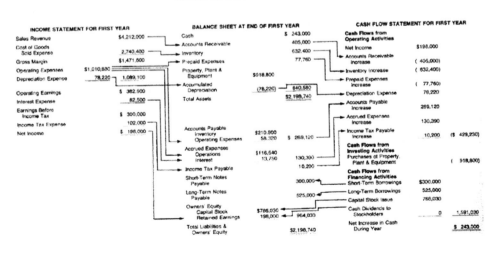

[11] *Id.* 20.

Projections

Projections are simply an estimate of what you think the financial statements of your business will look like for some future period. You develop projections based on certain assumptions about the progress of your business. Assumptions are based on sound research and analysis and identify the milestones you want to achieve at various points in your business' future. Finally, you map the projections to your milestones to determine the capital you will need to achieve your goals and when you will need the capital.

Said another way, projections are simply the quantification of your business plan. They are the way that a company without a history can make an educated guess about its future development.

Projections should tell your story in numbers as clearly as your business plan tells your story in words.

I believe there are three elements that will make projections solid and believable.

First, under-promise and over-deliver. Companies seldom meet or exceed their initial forecasts. Entrepreneurs provide forecasts they think investors want to see. In an article called "The Art of Projections in a Dotcom 2.0 World,"[12] Guy Kawasaki encourages entrepreneurs to use the following rule of thumb: "Divide your sales forecasts by 100 and add one year to projected shipping dates for startups without a prototype and for a startup with a prototype, divide your sales forecasts by ten and add six months to your projected shipping dates."

Second, be confident. You need to be sure about your numbers and be able to articulate them with a good and believable story.

Third, base your projections on good and solid "assumptions." What exactly is an assumption? An "assumption" is a fact that is presumed to be true without

---

[12] Guy Kawasaki, *The Art of Projections in a Dotcom 2.0 World*, How to Change the World (Nov. 2, 2006), http://blog.guykawasaki.com/2006/11/the_art_of_proj.html.

conclusive evidence. It is an educated guess used to project numbers for a business with no previous history. However, you want to base your assumptions on any relevant data you have. Assumptions should be made about the following sorts of things: your business model, the market for your products or services, development of the product or service, your competition, costs of manufacturing and production, and operating costs.

It is critical to develop the assumptions on which you will base your projections together with your team so that each member contributes and takes ownership of the model you develop.

A startup needs to balance the time requirement to actually get to market and the expectations of investors who likely have a limited time frame for investment.

To properly develop projections, your business must sell or be planning to sell something. It must produce and deliver the product or service, incur costs to do so, and acquire assets.

Again, using Guy Kawasaki's advice, he says to develop projections, focus on two or three key metrics that drive growth, revenues, and expenses. You can think of these three elements as buckets on which you can build your projections.

Growth: Items you need to enable a business to scale. Matters related to growth include elements of both revenues and expenses.

Revenue: Items directly related to increasing the top-line results of your business.

Expenses: Items that decrease your net income and are the costs to run your business. You need to show an investor that you understood both the economics and evolution of the growth and scale of your company including that this belief is grounded in reality.

Think about the following:

What is your market? What problem does your product or service address? What is the solution it provides to the problem? Is there something special about your particular value proposition or your timing to get to market? Who is in your customer profile and target market, and how strong and deep is your customer pipeline? Consider revenue, head count, real estate (if any), and distribution/inventory costs. These are all things that help you to grow and scale your business.

If you believe you can increase revenue, do you need to increase your cost of goods sold at the same time? How might you be able to increase your margins by decreasing your costs of goods sold? How can your operating costs be minimized? Figure out the number of sales you need to close for your company to begin to have net profit and from there work backwards to determine the number of production lines needed to ship orders to meet those goals. Is there a niche or market on which you intend to focus that might draw in more customers?

In "How to Create a Financial Forecast," Kawasaki advises to "show investors how you will grow your company from the bottom up—sale by sale, employee by employee—rather than building a model from the top down. No one believes that a model built on getting 'only one percent of the target market' is a credible plan."[13] Building a model from the bottom up is often referred to as a reverse income statement. For example, instead of assuming you can get one percent of the market share for your business, figure out how many business development and sales meetings you believe you can have each week. Then multiply that number by the percentage you think will be successful. Then add six months to close a sale.

Begin your initial work on your projections by developing a "reverse income statement." Specify how much revenue is expected, what your COGS is projected to be, the return on assets necessary to make the business profitable, and the maximum assets needed for the venture. Begin by projecting the before tax profit you would like to achieve, your return on investment, what your unit of business is, and the average price per unit.

---

[13] Read more at: Guy Kawasaki, *How to Create an Enchanting Financial Forecast #OfficeandGuyK*, HOW TO CHANGE THE WORLD (Jan. 17, 2012), http://blog.guykawasaki.com/2012/01/how-to-create-an-enchanting-financial-forecast-officeandguyk.html#ixzz2qDVEQR7Z.

You and your team should constantly review your historical and projected numbers and assess the following: How successful were you at reaching your targets, how did your budget compare with actual numbers, how many days did it take to close a deal, what is your average deal size, what were your average receivables aging, how long do you hold payables before paying?

In addition to putting together a reverse income statement, you need to put together a development schedule for your product, offering or service. You need to base the development schedule on realistic assumptions. Figure out the significant milestones associated with your company's offering. Investors will be looking for the various points in your plan that will add value to your company and could result in the value of the company increasing. Again, Kawasaki would tell you not to confuse milestones, assumptions, and tasks. Milestones are the things a company must do to achieve its goals (e.g., make x amount of sales, sign x amount of customers). Assumptions are those things that are educated guesses that form the basis of your projections and enable you to develop your financial plan (e.g., barrier to entry in this segment is low; no other company meeting need of niche). Tasks are things like renting an office, buying supplies—things that must be done to accomplish your milestones.

Once you have developed your milestones, examine your funding requirements to reach your milestones. Develop a list that shows the funding requirements needed to reach each milestone. Such a map gives investors a complete picture of the funds you think you need to reach the milestones you have projected.

The Real World

Beth Leonard, managing partner at the accounting firm Lurie Besikoff Lapidus & Co, often starts her talks about the need for financials with the following real-life anecdote: She was attending a Vikings/Packers game many years ago and during the halftime a small town marching band came onto the field. Beth immediately turned to her boyfriend/now husband and said, "There are 276 students in that marching band. This must be the biggest trip that band has made in years." Her husband looked at her incredulously. "How did I know the number of students and figure out their story?" she said. "I counted the rows and columns of students and multiplied to determine how many people in the band and then read where they were from on the scoreboard and made my deductions from there." Similarly, every financial statement and projection must tell a story.

In addition, Beth explained that consistency in developing financial statements is essential. You must make sure an investor can trust that you are producing your financial statements using the same rules each time so that the story you tell can be easily and confidently extrapolated.

Takeaways from Chapter 3

- *First*, understand what comprises a financial statement: (1) the balance sheet: a "snapshot" of the assets and liabilities of the company at a specific moment in time, (2) the income statement: a summary of sales, net profit, expenses, and net income over a specific period of time, and (3) the cash flow statement: the inflows and outflows of cash over a specific period of time.
- *Second*, make projections (assumptions) about the progress of the company and map those projections to the company's existing milestones and development schedule to determine the capital the company will need to achieve its goals.
- *Third*, regarding projections, (1) under-promise and over-deliver, (2) be confident, and (3) base projections on sound assumptions.
- *Fourth*, focus on key metrics that drive growth, revenues, and expenses.
- *Fifth*, begin initial work on financial projections by developing a "reverse income statement."
- *Sixth*, engage the company's team to ensure each team member contributes and takes ownership of the projections developed.
- *Seventh*, constantly review historical and projected financial information to assess and improve accuracy.

4

Organization and Structure

*"Two roads diverged in a yellow wood,
and sorry I could not travel both." - Robert Frost*

Recently I had a new client call me and ask me to work with her and her business partner to develop a new company. She said to me in our first call, "We know we want to organize as a corporation in Nevada." Then I began to ask the following questions:

- *What is your endgame?*
- *Do you want pass-through income?*
- *Do you intend to seek investors or self-fund?*
- *Will you have one, or more than one, bricks-and-mortar offices?*
- *Will you have an office in Nevada?*

The client had not thought about any of these questions, and did not understand how they impacted her decision about where to organize and what type of entity to form.

Entrepreneurs are much better off thinking about the answers to these types of questions rather than deciding what type of entity to form and where to organize.

To answer the question, "What is your endgame?" entrepreneurs need to consider whether they hope to grow a business to sell, to leave for children to run or to assist them to maintain their lifestyle over a long period of time.

An entrepreneur will be better off identifying his or her goals first and then consulting with counsel to use those goals to inform the decision about the type of entity to form and where to organize.

Type of Entity to Form

There are several factors entrepreneurs should consider before they decide the type of entity to form for their business. Among them are the following:

- *Number of Owners: Some entities have limits on the number of owners.*
- *Will owners be individuals, corporations, trusts, etc.: Certain entities can be owned only by individuals and certain trusts.*
- *What is the over-arching goal of the business: Growing and scaling a business or running a lifestyle business will impact the type of entity you form.*
- *How will the business be capitalized: If the owners plan to accept investment by outside investors, consider the type of entities that will invest—i.e., individuals or funds.*
- *Do owners want pass-through income taxation: Consider what will be the most attractive tax approach for the owners, and if applicable, the investors. Do the owners and/or investors want pass-through losses (likely in early years) and income that will be reported in his, her or its personal return?*
- *Ability to retain earnings without owners being taxed: Do the owners want to be able to retain profits in the company without having to pay tax on them?*
- *Do the owners want to participate in employee benefit plans? Certain structures will not allow owners to participate as employees.*
- *Do owners want to distribute profits disparately among them? Certain structures require owners to split all profits equally. Other structures allow much more flexibility.*

Types of Entities and Impact of Above Factors

1. S Corporations:

A corporation that makes a valid election to be taxed under Subchapter S of Chapter 1 of the Internal Revenue Code is treated as a pass-through entity for tax purposes.

An S corporation can only be owned by individuals and certain kinds of trusts. In addition, an S corporation cannot be owned by more than one hundred individuals who must be US citizens or resident aliens. An S corporation provides protection to its owners by limiting their liability so that the personal assets of the owners cannot be seized to pay obligations of the business.

S corporations' owners are called shareholders. An S corporation can only issue one class of stock to its owners, although this one class can be divided into voting and non-voting shares.

S corporation shareholders can at the same time be employees of the company and draw salaries from the company. The salaries paid are not subject to self-employment tax liability even if paid by an S corporation to an owner of the corporation.

2.   C Corporations:

Any corporation that is taxed separately from its owners is a "C" corporation under the Internal Revenue Code. A C corporation differs from an S corporation in several ways.

There is no limit on the type of individuals or entities that can own stock of a C corporation. The C corporation is itself a taxed entity and the stockholders are paid dividends on which they must pay income tax; this is often referred to as "double taxation." A C corporation can have any number of classes of shares. If a company intends to capitalize using venture capital money, investors from the West Coast often insist on C corporation structure.

3.   Limited Liability Companies

A limited liability company has certain characteristics that are similar to an S corporation and other characteristics that make it quite different. Like S corporations, limited liability companies (LLC) are taxed as pass-through entities and thus each owner (called a "member") must report his, her or its share of income or loss on a personal tax return. Members can be any type of person or entity, similar to the shareholders of a C corporation. An LLC can have multiple classes of interests (like stock).

However, its owners who are active in the business cannot be employees like in an S corporation. Instead they receive guaranteed payments and must pay self-employment tax on the amounts received. LLCs can also distribute profits on a disproportionate basis to owners with more flexibility than other types of organizational entities.

Where to Organize

In starting a new business, entrepreneurs must not only determine the type of business entity that will best suit their needs, but must choose a state in which to organize the entity. Founders of a business must consider the following factors before they make a decision regarding where to file their organizational papers:

- *State income tax laws*
- *Development of business laws in a state*
- *Investor preference*
- *Founder goals*
- *Where main business office will be located*

State Income Tax Laws

Entrepreneurs often think they are better off organizing their entity in a state like Nevada or Florida that has no state income tax. This may be true if the bulk of the company's revenue will come from the state that has no state income tax. However, if that is not the case, the entity still must pay state income tax in those states in which it does business. In addition, the entity will have to pay administrative costs to maintain an agent for service of process in the state of registration as well as qualifying to do business in the state(s) in which it operates. Therefore, organizing in a state where a business has no connection simply because the state has no income tax is not a wise business decision.

State Laws Relating to Business

Entrepreneurs often think that the state of Delaware is a good place to organize. In fact, Delaware has a very well developed body of corporate law and the courts that hear business cases do not have juries, only judges. However, unless your business will have an office in Delaware or you have investors who insist on a Delaware corporation, it will be cheaper and easier initially to organize in the state where your main office will be located.

Investor Preference

If a company intends to seek venture capital financing from firms that are not located in the state in which the company is located, then organizing in Delaware may be a good choice because the environment and laws are very favorable to businesses.

****

The state in which a company organizes is not a final decision, however. It is possible to merge an entity organized in one state into an entity organized in another state if that becomes more desirable. However, changing company form could be more difficult. It is problematic to convert from a C corp to an S corp. If the company is sold before it has been an S corp for ten years, there are certain additional taxes that will be required to be paid (called "built in gains"). It is fairly easy, however, to convert an LLC to a corporation if new investors insist or the company seeks to go public.

The Real World

Todd Rooke, the co-CEO of Jingit, LLC, explained that the company he co-founded with Joe Rogness was originally named 7 Ventures, LLC. They did not exactly know what they would ultimately name the company but wanted to make sure they had set up a limited liability company structure in Delaware. Many high-tech companies and payment companies organize in Delaware. Their goal was to merge the payment space and the advertising space and they believed that organizing in Delaware would serve them well. They ultimately changed the name of the company to Jingit because it matched their business model, which paid consumers to watch advertisements.

Todd also advises that it is important for every business to go through various pivots. As you are validating your business hypothesis, the more nimble you can be, the faster your business will develop.

Takeaways from Chapter 4

Entrepreneurs should consider the below factors in determining the type of entity to form.

Consideration	S-Corporation	C-Corporation	Limited Liability Company
How many owners?	Can only be owned by 100 or less individuals	No limit on number	No limit on number
Are the owners individuals, corporations or trusts?	Can only be owned by certain trusts or individuals (US citizens or resident aliens)	No limit on type of individual or entity	No limit on type of individual or entity
How will the business be capitalized?		Venture capital investors from the West Coast often insist on this structure	
Do the owners want pass-through income taxation?	Pass through entity for taxation	Entity and stockholder paid dividends are both taxed: double taxation	Pass through entity for taxation
Do the owners want to be able to retain profits in the company without paying taxes on them?	Owners can also be employees and draw salaries from the company; the salaries are not subject to self-employment tax liability	Owners pay taxes on profits	Owners cannot be employees Receive payments as owners and must report income/loss on personal tax return

Do the owners want to participate in employee benefit plans?	No restriction on owner participation	No restriction on owner participation	Owners of an LLC cannot participate in its employee benefit plans
Do the owners want to distribute profits disparately?	Cannot distribute profits disproportionately	Cannot distribute profits disproportionately	May distribute profits disproportionately
What type of ownership structure is desired?	Owners are shareholders and only one class of stock can be issued to the owners, although it can be divided between voting and nonvoting	Owners are shareholders and any number of classes of shares is permitted	Owners are members and any number of classes of shares is permitted
Do owners want limited liability?	Limited liability of owners	Limited liability of owners	Limited liability of owners

5

Splitting Equity

"Motivational compatibility does not guarantee success but incompatibility is asking for trouble." - Noam Wasserman

One of the most important things founders do in a startup business is to split the equity among them. There are many considerations that founders need to think about in connection with dividing equity. These include: 1) how much equity to give each founder; 2) will one or more of the founders be awarded more equity because he or she came up with the idea for the company; 3) what type of equity will be granted to each of the founders; and 4) when will the equity be divided among the founders.

Split Considerations

Founders of a company generally join together because they have some sort of collective vision about creating an entity. Sometimes founders know each other in advance, and sometimes they have met only in connection with the company they seek to build. Entering into a relationship with others to build a company is like a marriage—and as we all know, there are good marriages and bad marriages. This chapter will help you consider the steps to take when splitting equity to avoid problems down the road.

Perhaps one of the most famous recent cases regarding equity splitting is *Facebook v. Saverin*.[14] In this case, Eduardo Saverin, who claimed to be one of the co-founders of Facebook, sued Facebook and Mark Zuckerberg because the parties did not have a clear agreement about what amount of

---

[14] Owen Thomas, *Facebook Founders Settle Their Feud* (Jan. 30, 2009), http://gawker.com/5143256/facebook-founders-settle-their-feud.

equity each would own in the Facebook business. There was no early documentation and disagreement about how the equity was divided at the onset. This case, more than many others in recent history, illustrates the need for founders to be clear about splitting a venture's equity.

Not all experts on founding companies agree, however, that equity should be split within the early days of the venture. Noah Wasserman in his book *The Founder's Dilemmas: Anticipating and Avoiding the Pitfalls That Can Sink a Startup*[15] suggests that founders carefully consider timing regarding when they want to split equity in a business. He posits that by waiting until after the business has been running for a period of time, the roles of the parties become clear, and the equity reward more apparent. He is right that oftentimes, when equity is split at the beginning of a venture, there are arguments later that the split was not equitable because of the roles the parties ultimately assume in the business.

The advantage to splitting equity at the beginning of the venture is that negotiations will likely be calmer and it is a way to attract and incentivize key founders. The disadvantage to splitting equity at the beginning of the venture is that, as the venture develops, the initial split may be unfair, and it is very hard to renegotiate thereafter. The advantage to splitting the equity later in the development of a venture is that the co-founders will learn more about each other and the startup strategy and the business model will be more solidified, the co-founders' commitments will be more apparent to all founders, and the founders will likely avoid renegotiations later on. The disadvantage to splitting the equity later in the development of a venture is that the cofounders may have very different views about the value they brought to the venture, which can cause extreme discord and even lawsuits. Alternatively, the founders could split a certain percentage of the equity early on and then leave a "pool" to split among them later.

The considerations founders should apply to determine how to split equity include a founder's contribution to the ideas of the new venture, his or her monetary contribution, and his or her commitment to involvement in the venture as it is being built. In addition, the opportunity costs to a founder

---

[15] NOAH WASSERMAN, THE FOUNDER'S DILEMMAS: ANTICIPATING AND AVOIDING THE PITFALLS THAT CAN SINK A STARTUP (2013).

should be considered. What did the founder forego to join the entity (e.g., a job with a guaranteed salary and/or bonus, other startup opportunities, etc.)? The founders should also consider what the future contribution of the founders will be to the venture. For example, will the person with the "idea" be involved as the entity develops, what is the level of commitment of each of the founders, and what roles will each of the founders play? It is also important to consider what a founder's motivations and preferences are. Is the founder motivated by wealth, risk tolerance or risk aversion, conflict tolerance or conflict avoidance, and how do the founder's past relationships influence his or her behavior? There are many assessments that can be used to determine some of these characteristics. One I particularly like can be found at http://www.authentichappiness.sas.upenn.edu.[16]

The considerations in splitting equity require honest and transparent discussions among the founders. My suggestion is that the founders must be absolutely clear about their relationships with each other and the manner in which the equity will be split. I am somewhat agnostic about when the equity should be split, but suggest that in any event it be done within the first six months of the founding of the company.

Character of Equity To Be Given To Founders

There is flexibility among the various forms of equity granted to founders. These include stock or member interests, restricted stock or options, or a combination of these forms of equity.

Straight Equity or Member Interests

Stock or member interests can be given to founders in exchange for cash contributions to the company. The character of these interests have no strings attached and give the founder an unencumbered piece of the company.

Restricted Stock

Often founders are also given "restricted stock or restricted member interests." These types of interests are "restricted" in the sense that the equity is subject to

---

[16] *Authentic Happiness*, PENN, http://www.authentichappiness.sas.upenn.edu.

a risk of forfeiture. Examples of "restrictions" include leaving the employ of the company, not achieving performance objectives, or a combination of the two. If the restriction is not met, then the founder loses the ownership of the units. This is a way to tie the founder to the company. Typically, restricted stock is taxed like income when it vests. However, the owner of restricted stock can file an election with the Internal Revenue Service under 26 U.S.C. § 83(b)[17] of the Internal Revenue Code (an "83B Election") to pay tax on the entire value of the stock at grant and not when it vests. The stock is generally of a lower value at grant than when it vests. In addition, receiving equity rather than options enables the founder to start the capital gains period for the stock at the time the equity is issued. Otherwise, when the restricted stock "vests" (i.e., no longer subject to a risk of forfeiture), the founder must pay ordinary income tax on the difference between the value at grant and the value at vesting. The disadvantage to an 83B Election is that the founder cannot take any sort of deduction or loss if the restrictions are not met and the stock never vests. In a startup situation this is often not a problem, however, since the tax paid initially is minimal.

Below is an example of how an 83B Election works and what the tax liability would be with and without the Election.[18]

You Don't Do Anything	You File 83(b) Election
Initial Grant - Company Value is $0.01/share	
Founder Pays No Tax **Total Tax Liability - $0.00**	Founder pays tax on two years worth of shares at present value **Total Tax Liability - $3.00**

---

[17] I.R.C. § 83(b) (2012).

[18] Steven Ayr, *What Is An 83(b) Election and When Do I Make It?*, THE LAW OFFICE OF STEVEN M. AYR (Feb. 26, 2013), http://ayrlaw.com/what-is-an-83b-election-and-when-do-i-make-it-part-1-with-graphic/.

End of Year 1 - Company Value is $10/share

Founder pays income tax on 500 shares valued at $10/share

Total Tax Liability -
$1,650.00

Founder retains vested shares, pays no additional tax

Total Tax Liability -
$3.00

End of Year 2 - Company Value is $100/share

Founder pays income tax on 500 shares valued at $100/share

Total Tax Liability -
$18,150.00

Founder retains vested shares, pays no additional tax

Total Tax Liability -
$3.00

Year 2.5 - Company Purchased at $150/Share - Founder Liquidates

Founder pays long term capital gains on 500 shares, short term capital gains on 500

Total Tax Liability -
$40,400.00

Founder pays long term capital gains on all 1000 shares

Total Tax Liability -
$30,003.00

Options

Stock or member interest options can also be given to founders. These types of interests vest upon the occurrence of certain events. Examples would be (i) the passage of time—i.e., the founder has remained a company employee for a period of time; (ii) achievement of performance goals; or (iii) a combination of remaining with the company *and* achieving performance goals. The disadvantage to giving founders options is that they are taxed as ordinary income when the options are exercised. Options are very good incentives to give to employees (see Chapter 9); however, they are less advantageous for founders because they will, in most circumstances, result in ordinary income tax on the difference between the value at exercise and the stock price.

The Real World

Two founders of an entity often decide to split the equity 50/50 between them. While that indicates a desire to be equal partners and operate the business collaboratively, it does not address what happens if circumstances go awry. Just as founding an entity is a marriage, it is critical for the parties to have a "prenuptial" agreement that provides a self-executing way to divorce from one another. These agreements are called "buy/sell" agreements, or if the entity is a limited liability company, a "member control agreement." It is important for the parties to determine what should happen if a founder dies, becomes disabled, acts in a way that requires he or she be terminated from working for the entity for "cause," or the entity is at an impasse about actions to take in the future. I have developed a questionnaire I give founders to facilitate discussion regarding these various situations. This allows the founders to do the preliminary work without counsel and then I review the questionnaire, discuss it with the founders, and prepare the agreement that reflects their desires. I have had clients who divide the equity equally among founders without regard to the role each plays in the company and founders who have given the founder with the idea an equity premium. Sometimes it is necessary to terminate a founder because he or she acts in a way that is detrimental to the company. It is best to execute such actions swiftly rather than waiting to "see what happens." Moreover, I have sometimes negotiated settlements with founders in these situations where they are permitted to retain some amount of stock in the company. In such a situation, I always recommend that the departing founder give an irrevocable proxy to one of the remaining founders to vote his or her shares. Doing so removes any problems to obtain the founder's agreement later when the company is sold.

Takeaways from Chapter 5

- *First, in determining when to split the equity of the company,* consider the costs and benefits of (1) splitting the equity of the company within the early days of the venture to ensure clarity and attract key founders, (2) splitting the equity later after the roles of each individual have become clearer and the equity can be divided most equitably, or (3) splitting some portion of the equity early and leaving a pool of equity to split later.

- *Second, in determining how to split the equity of the company,* consider the following factors for each individual founder: (1) contributions to the ideas for the venture; (2) monetary contributions; (3) time commitment and involvement; (4) opportunity costs; (5) potential future contributions and roles; (5) motivations and preferences (e.g., risk/conflict/wealth tolerance and aversion); and (6) past relationships' influence on behavior.

- *Third, in determining the character of equity* to be given to the founders, consider the costs and benefits of and the incentives created by each of the following forms of equity: (1) stock or member interests that have no strings attached and provide the founder an unencumbered piece of the company; (2) restricted stock that ties the founder to the company by creating restrictions that if violated cause the founder to lose the stock (e.g., performance, leaving employ of the company); (3) options that tie the founder to the company by tying the vesting of the stock to certain events (e.g., duration of employment with the company, achievement of performance goals); and (4) combinations of these forms.

- *Fourth, in determining the proportions of equity* to be given to each founder, determine what will happen in the event a founder dies, becomes disabled, acts in a way that requires termination for cause, or the company is at an impasse about actions to take in the future.

6

Branding

"A designer knows that he has achieved perfection not when there is nothing left to add, but when there is nothing left to take away."
- Antoine de Saint-Exupéry

Branding is the way in which a business identifies its customer and determines its brand promise regarding its product or services. A well-developed brand both attracts customers and keeps them as a consumer of its product or service.

Developing a Brand Promise

To develop an effective brand promise an entrepreneur must consider the following four elements:

- *Target market (Ask: Who is it?)*
- *Definition of your market (Ask: What is it?)*
- *Rational or emotional benefit of the brand promise (Ask: What will the customers receive from my promise?)*
- *The reason consumers should believe the brand promise (Ask: Why should a customer believe my promise?)*

I advised earlier in Chapter 2 the need to focus on the product or service your business will sell. Similarly, the classic way to develop a brand promise is to look at the four elements above and answer the questions set forth next to each element.

In developing a brand for a new company, "less is more." The more focused your brand is, the easier it will be to determine and develop your brand promise. I often see companies begin with grandiose ideas about all the world's ills they want to save and their brand promises are just as broad. However, after they get into the development stage, successful companies realize the need to focus.

Focus on your initial target market and later consider whether or not you may be able to expand. Focus will enable you to begin faster, easier, and better.

Monica Skipper, brand strategy team lead at Fed Ex, put it very simply: Know who you are, be who you are, say who you are. In terms of Fed Ex, this advice would mean the following: Fed Ex's brand promise is reliability. According to Ms. Skipper, if your brand promise is "reliability," then "you need to offer reliability in everything you do—from your products and services to your website and communications." Ms. Skipper advises to "say who you are over and over again." She concludes by saying, "Before you get caught up in wordsmithing, font choices and color palettes, ask yourself: Why am I in this business to begin with? What is my unique benefit to customers? If you want your small business to grow and thrive, you need to know the answers. And always keep your promises."

Examples of three excellent brand promises that illustrate the above points are the following:

- *The NFL:* "To be the premier sports and entertainment brand that brings people together, connecting them socially and emotionally like no other."
- *Coca-Cola:* "To inspire moments of optimism and uplift."
- *Virgin:* "To be genuine, fun, contemporary, and different in everything we do at a reasonable price."

Note that none of these brand promises speaks to what the company actually does. But these brand promises do speak to the attributes of what these companies promise to their consumers. These attributes are the following:

- *The NFL:* Integrity, excellence, community, teamwork, innovation, tradition.

- *Coca-Cola:* Simple pleasures, optimism, happiness, human connections/ bringing people together.
- *Virgin:* Fun, rebellion, self-expression, rock-star-lifestyle quality (at accessible cost).

A strong brand promise should then inform all the decisions a company makes. Looking again at the three examples above:

- *The NFL* uses its brand promise (including its values and attributes) to choose subjects for commercials, determine what to approve as official/licensed apparel and what to offer as sanctioned souvenirs, and who to invite as halftime entertainment. (Thus its horror at a halftime snafu a few years ago, for which it apologized profusely.)
- *Coca-Cola* has become one of the strongest brands in the world through making strategic business decisions based on its brand promise, from what products it offers to how it offers them. For most of us, it is easiest to see Coca-Cola living its promise through the commercials it chooses to air: Commercials like the ones showing "scary" football star Mean Joe Green turning friendly after a young boy gives him his drink[19] and people from disparate countries coming together to "teach the world to sing."[20]
- *Virgin* uses its brand promise across all its separate divisions— divisions as disparate as Virgin Balloon Flights, health clubs (Virgin Active), and financial services (Virgin Money). Its gyms have tons of extras and fun amenities, its financial services business focuses on taking complex products and making them easy to understand and accessibly priced, and its balloon flights are—no explanation needed!

(All of the above examples are taken from FrogDog.[21])

---

[19] *Coca-Cola 'Mean Joe Greene',* YOUTUBE, https://www.youtube.com/watch?v=-oaiV8MQH7s (uploaded Jan. 16, 2009).
[20] *Coca Cola Commercial- I'd Like to Teach the World to Sing (In Perfect Harmony)- 1971,* YOUTUBE, https://www.youtube.com/watch?v=ib-Qiyklq-Q (uploaded Dec. 29, 2008).
[21] *Brands are Promises,* FROGDOG, http://frog-dog.com/articles/detail/brands_are_promises/ (last visited June 18, 2014).

According to Guy Kawasawki in "The Art of the Start," part of developing a great brand is starting with a product or service that is great. Guy believes that the quota for making mistakes with a great product or service is much higher than products or services that are not, in his words, "inherently contagious." By this he means, cool, effective, distinctive, emotive, disruptive, deep, indulgent, and/or supported.

Developing a Creative Brief

After the brand and messages are developed, it is necessary to develop a creative brief, which provides the advertising strategy for how to execute on the brand. The creative brief is sometimes developed by an advertising agency, but with startups often this task is left to the founders. The creative brief should use the development work done with the brand and answer the following questions:

- *Who do we want to sell to? (Target)*
- *What are we selling? (Benefit)*
- *Why should they believe us? (Reason to believe)*
- *What do we want the advertising to do? (Strategy)*
- *What do we want people to do? (Response)*
- *What do we want people to feel? (Brand equity)*[22]

The Real World

Lloyd Sigel, former CEO of Lloyd's Barbeque Company, is a branding expert extraordinaire. He cautions that brands must be "instantly intuitive." Otherwise, in a world where time is money, it will take a consumer too long to understand your brand and even longer to decide if he or she wants to use it. If your business has a product or service that is hard to differentiate from others, in Lloyd's words, it is "ubiquitous," then it is very challenging to create brand differentiation. It is for that reason he believes that a brand must be "instantly intuitive." According to Lloyd, if you have to ask what a business does after hearing its name, choose another name!

---

[22] Graham Robertson, *How to Write an Effective Creative Brief*, BELOVED BRANDS (May 28, 2012), http://beloved-brands.com/2012/05/28/creative-brief/.

The Legal Part of Branding

A trademark is defined as "a symbol, word, or words legally registered or established by use as representing a company or product." A trademark not only distinguishes the goods or services of your company but assures consumers of their quality and enables you to advertise and promote your products in a short-hand way.

The first party who uses a trademark, whether or not it has been registered, has the right to exclude use of confusingly similar marks by a later user. Of course, the first party must be able to prove that the trademark has been used and that the combination of words is sufficiently unique to be considered a trademark. This is done by showing evidence of the first use of the trademark in advertisements, on websites, business cards, and on the product itself. The timing of when to register a trademark depends. A trademark cannot be registered until it is used. However, waiting too long to register a trademark might result in developing brand equity in a mark that has been used by someone else (see Chapter 11).

Takeaways from Chapter 6

- *First, focus on the customers* to determine how to shape the company's brand and the reasons the target customers should believe in the company's brand promise.
- *Second, focus on a narrow and discrete target market* to create a strong brand and, if possible, expand later.
- *Third,* promise the company's brand is and will be what it claims to be and *keep that promise* to inspire consumer loyalty and confidence in the brand.
- *Fourth, inform all decision making with the brand promise* to ensure stability of the brand.
- *Fifth, remember the product and service have to begin and continue to be great* to develop a strong and effective brand message.
- *Sixth, develop a creative brief* that provides the advertising and marketing strategy for how to execute the brand.
- *Seventh, register a trademark for its brand symbol or words representing the brand* to protect your intellectual property rights in the brand.

7

Valuation

"We do not see things as they are, nor do we even see them as we are, but only as we believe our story to have been."
- Eric Michael Leventhal

Entrepreneurs often wonder how to value their companies. They look for a formula or template or magic bullet to determine a methodology. However, the answer, as with many things in the world of startups, is "it depends."

There are many terms you might have heard in valuation discussions. These include "Discounted Cash Flow" analysis (often referred to as DCF), "Market Transaction Variables" analysis, and "Book Value/Liquidation Value" analysis. This chapter will demystify these terms and educate you to talk with possible investors confidently.

If your company is revenue producing, there are formulas you can use to help with valuation. Oftentimes, revenue producing companies are sold at multiples of EBITDA (earnings before interest, taxes and depreciation) (see Chapter 3). Different industries may have different multiples depending on several factors, including whether the company in question is a leading or lagging indicator in terms of economic growth and what is the then-current state of the economy.

Discounted Cash Flow Analysis

A discounted cash flow analysis uses projections of the future value of a company and then "discounts" them to current value based on the fact that money has a time value and is worth less today than in the future. The steps in a discounted cash flow analysis are explained in the article, *Valuation 101: How to Do a Discounted Cashflow Analysis.*[23]

Market Transaction Variables Analysis

To determine a company's value based on comparable companies, you compare one or more aspects of your company to the same aspects of other companies that have established market values. The challenge to do this sort of analysis for privately held companies is that the information most readily available for comparison purposes is for publicly held companies. A simple example is if comparable companies have EBITDA of $1mm and have sold at multiples of five, then the value of your company should be approximately five times the EBITDA of your company.

Book Value Per Share

Calculating book value will almost always give you a lower value than any other formula. This calculation is done by subtracting the company's liabilities on its balance sheet from its assets on its balance sheet. To determine the per share book value, simply divide the number obtained from the preceding formula by the number of shares then outstanding.

Liquidation Value

The liquidation value of a company is generally determined by the sum of its physical assets as set forth on its balance sheet. The value of each physical asset is equal to its original cost minus depreciation.

Startup's Value

Most startups do not have revenue and therefore the traditional methods of calculating value referenced will not be overly helpful.

Alok Patnia in a quote in YOUR STORY in December 2013 suggested that valuation of startups is dependent on the following:

---

[23] *Valuation 101: How to Do a Discounted Cashflow Analysis,* STOCKOPEDIA (Jan. 22, 2012), http://www.stockopedia.com/content/valuation-101-how-to-do-a-discounted-cashflow-analysis-63489/.

The biggest determinant of your startup's value are the market forces of the industry and sector in which it plays, which include the balance (or imbalance) between demand and supply of money, the timeliness and size of recent exits, the willingness for an investor to pay a premium to get into a deal, and the level of desperation of the entrepreneur looking for money.[24]

If we unpack Patnia's statement, he indicates there is no real formula, but rather the market forces at work in your startups' industry, recency and size of exits, and willingness of an investor to pay a premium.

The market forces that may affect an investor's willingness to invest will depend on whether the market is then depressed or booming. If the market is depressed, an investor is *likely* to pay less to invest in your company *unless* the investor has confidence that the market will shift or he or she is willing to take a risk because of some other company factor. This other factor most likely would be confidence in the human capital that is associated with the company or the view that the idea truly meets an unmet need and will quickly gain traction.

If the market in your industry is booming, then an investor may be *likely* to invest at a premium *because* of his or confidence in the company (including of course its human capital), as well as confidence that the industry will continue to thrive.

There are times when a startup can command a premium from those who want to invest. How do entrepreneurs create such a situation? Conventional wisdom is that there are four factors that will influence whether or not an investor will agree to pay a premium. I have found these factors to be important in the decisions made by investors. The first of these factors is the sector of the startup. Certain sectors are perceived by investors as being "hot," and thus there will be competition for the ability to invest. The second factor that influences investors to pay a premium is the human capital that is running the business. As I have said elsewhere in this book, investors invest

---

[24] *See* Alok Patnia, *How does an Investor Value a Startup*, YOUR STORY (Dec. 10, 2013), http://yourstory.com/2013/12/startup-valuation/.

in people, rather than ideas. So a great management team will draw investors like a bee to honey. The third factor is a functioning product where the investors have a proof of concept. Trying to raise money early in a startup is always challenging. Investors want to see that the product has been proven, yet the company needs money to develop the proof of concept. However, to negotiate from a position of strength, founders are best to have objective proof that their idea will work. Finally, the fourth factor that will influence investors is the traction of the product. If the investor has been able to attract early adopters who have tried the product and will recommend its success, investors may compete to invest in the company.

The recency and size of exits have an impact on how a potential investor values your company. Investors look at many deals every day. This is the lens through which they form a mental picture of what constitutes an "average" size round/investment, an average price, and the average amount of money your company will need relative to others in the space in which it operates. To the extent you can understand the lens through which the investor is evaluating your company, the better you will be at discussing the valuation of your company with the potential investor. Investors also use recent exits to model their valuation of your company. The value placed on a company by an entrepreneur is only useful to the extent such value coincides with the valuation of a possible investor.

The exit prices of comparable transactions will help the investor to model the internal rate of return they will achieve by investing in your company. To calculate the percentage they will receive in an investment, the investor will divide the post-money calculation of the business by the amount they invest and the quotient will be their percentage, assuming there are no other dilutive events. Although subsequent investments and valuations generally dilute the early investors' ownership percentage, they create higher value for all investors (i.e., the pie gets bigger and the piece of pie owned by an early investor may get smaller).

Finally, there are nonfinancial issues that affect the value of a company such as contractual rights (i.e., investors receiving preemptive rights, certain rights regarding non-dilution, board rights, and certain covenants from the company about how they will perform). In addition, the capital structure of a company itself can influence an investor in its valuation if the investor will receive a higher return on its investment than earlier investors. I have had companies that have drafted agreements providing for rounds of investment before the investment is made. An example of this type of future structure would be to insert the rights to a Series B preferred stock into the company's governing documents before the company actually issues the Series B preferred stock. I have done this with companies when an early investor may make the company a loan that is convertible into a future series at the time of the next investment in the company. In addition, investors may require they be provided with redemption rights exercisable after a specific period of time (these provide exit opportunities for the investor even if the company has not been sold). It is critical to carefully review the terms demanded by the investor and seek counsel to negotiate them. See Chapter 8 for a discussion of convertible loans.

Jargon

The terms "pre-money" and "post-money" are often used in discussing possible investment scenarios. Very simply, "pre-money" is the value of a company prior to an investment, and "post-money" is the value of the company after an investment. In large part, both the pre-money and post-money values are a result of the negotiations between the founders and the investors as to what percentage of the company the investors' dollars will buy.

For example, if the pre-money value of the company is $1,000,000 and the investor invests $500,000 in the company, then the post-money value of the company is $1,500,000 and the investor owns 1/3 of the company (500,000/1,500,000 = 33.33 percent). If the investor in the preceding scenario invests $1,000,000 then the post-money value is $2,000,000 and the founders and investors each own 50 percent ($1,000,000/$2,000,000 = 50 percent).

Let us see how the preceding calculations affect an exit. The exit calculation is determined by the following formula: exit value/percentage ownership = return. So in the preceding examples, assuming the company is sold for $5,000,000 then the investors who hold one-third of the company will receive $1,665,000 ($5,000,000/33.3 percent) and the investors who hold 50 percent will receive $2,500,000 ($5,000,000/50 percent).

If an entrepreneur is lucky enough to have investors competing to invest then he or she can be discriminating about who to tap as a future partner. The entrepreneur will be wise to evaluate whether or not the investors will also add value to the company. This value-add can come in the form of connections to distribution and/or sales networks, additional investors, strategies, and general advocacy of the company's product or service.

The Real World

Leslie Frecon, CEO of LFE Capital, provides expansion capital to companies as they are growing and scaling. Her hope is that the money her firm invests will help a company to become self-sustaining and revenue producing.

Leslie believes (and rightly so, I would contend) that companies need more than just capital—they need expertise. Such investors can help a company by providing access to resources that a company cannot tap into by itself. Firms like LFE Capital will work directly with management teams to bring the needed expertise to grow the company. Her team works with companies to develop projections and a viable business plan and then execute on the plan. LFE Capital will generally require a board seat on the board of companies in which the fund invests so as to have oversight, as well as input into, its development.

Leslie advises that she looks for the following elements when reviewing a business plan:

1. Description of the product or service;
2. Description and quantification of the market and market opportunity;
3. How to go to market;
4. Competition;
5. How the business will make money;
6. Historical financials and projections; and
7. Who are the likely buyers of the business.

It is critically important that the business plan presented to an investor focus on how the investor will achieve a successful rate of return. The business plan is a company's raison d'etre and must convince an investor of its reason for being.

Takeaways from Chapter 7

- *First*, understand traditional valuation methods to appreciate how to value a company that does have revenue.
- *Second*, consider a combination of factors including industry market-forces, timing and size of exits, and willingness of investors to pay premiums rather than traditional valuation methods to determine the value of a company that does not have revenue.
- *Third*, understand how investors think about valuation in terms of the most recent exits of other companies in the same industry.
- *Fourth*, remember that nonfinancial issues, including the company's capital structure and contract rights, and preemptive rights, non-dilution rights, board rights, and performance promises often influence the valuation of a company.
- *Fifth*, learn financial jargon such as pre-money and post-money and the calculations that express such jargon to better talk to and understand investors.
- *Sixth*, capitalize on the four factors that influence whether investors will be willing to pay a premium: (1) the sector or industry of the company; (2) the human capital running the business; (3) the functioning product that shows investors the proof of concept; and (4) the traction of the product.
- *Seventh*, evaluate whether or not each investor, and investors in general, will add value to the company beyond the dollar amount of the investment to have the best chance of leveraging dollars invested.
- *Eighth*, show investors a business plan that demonstrates how the company will make money and earn the investor a successful rate of return to convince investors they want to invest in the company.

8

Adding Value, Adding Risks

"What most people underestimate is the emotional impact of having to answer to someone." - Michael Golden

There are many articles, videos, and even entire books written about the proper way to make a pitch to investors. But why take money from outsiders in the first place? I have found that entrepreneurs often concentrate on making the perfect pitch without understanding the consequences of taking money from outsiders. They do not assess the pros and cons of partnering with others who provide financial support. Understanding the impact of outside investment, after the investment is made, is too late.

What Taking Outside Money Means

Accepting money from others to help fund your business means you now have one or more partners—and like all partnerships you need to have done your homework and understand the impact such partners will have on your company. Once you accept money from others, your company is no longer solely your own. You no longer have the right to control everything. In fact, depending on how you organize your board (see Chapter 10) you may leave your position with your company vulnerable and open to termination. I have seen these situations and more. One company I worked with organized an initial board consisting only of independent members. None of the board members had invested in the company; their only equity came from the options they received for board service. The founder, as the CEO of the company, reported to the board of directors. Because the founder did not have majority control of the board, he left himself open to the board, without much skin in the game, regulating his compensation as well as his very existence and roles with the company. Ultimately, the founder exercised his power as the then current majority equity owner in the company to terminate the board members and thus mitigate in the only way he could the possibility that his independent board might terminate him from running his own company. Moral of this story: Be very careful and strategic about who is on your board of directors.

Before a founder decides to take investment from early investors, it is critical that the entrepreneur mitigate risk when accepting outside money by doing appropriate due diligence and selecting the right investor. Just because an investor's money is green, the investor is not necessarily the right fit for the company. Remember the product you are selling to an investor is the return on investment in your company. Of course, it is critical that an investor be interested, albeit passionate, about your product or service, but the bottom line for investors is that the bottom line of your company must bring them an adequate return on their investment.

Angel Investors

Develop a list of due diligence questions to ask investors to help gage their interest and commitment to your company. Here are a few examples:

- *What do they know about your industry?*
- *Describe the exits they have had from companies either in your industry or other industries? What were the specific exit events and did they consider the exits successful?*
- *Describe other boards of privately held companies on which they have served previously and provide examples of the assistance they provided to those companies.*
- *How will they use their connections to help you with distribution of your product or service and/or another round of investment?*
- *Will they give you references of other entrepreneurs in whose companies they have invested?*

The first round of investment in a startup after "friends and family" is generally composed of angel investors—high net worth individuals who are willing to take risks on early funding in startup companies. Some angels insist on a board seat and being involved in a company; others, after doing their due diligence, may make an investment and you will never hear from them again.

I have seen many situations where high net worth individuals invest in companies without understanding the landscape of the startup. As a result, much time and wheel-spinning is spent answering this type of investor's questions because the investor lacks startup experience. The investor may then insist on provisions in documents or prolong board discussions that do not apply to startups, though the issues such potential investors raise may have been quite applicable to the company or companies in which the investor made his or her money. Consider asking others who have experience working with startups—i.e., professionals such as lawyers or accountants, or mentors who have grown successful angel funded companies—to interview your potential investors.

There are many avenues to find the right investors in a company. (A new type of business might be a "Match.com" between entrepreneurs and investors—one that really works!) By using research tools on the Internet, such as LinkedIn, Facebook and other types of social media, and attending trade group meetings and industry conferences, find the investors that align with your passion, have experience in your industry or with distribution or sales in a similarly situated industry, and have the time to be involved. Warm introductions are critical. Find a way to connect to the investors you want to pitch.

Pitching

There are many good articles on pitching. Guy Kawasaki's advice[25] is excellent on how to create an "enchanting pitch." I recommend you review and follow his advice. In addition, practice your pitch so many times that you could deliver it in your sleep. Keep it simple. Tell stories shortly and succinctly. Use pictures rather than words. (It is true in this arena that a

---

[25] Guy Kawasaki, *How to Create an Enchanting Pitch #OfficeGuyK*, HOW TO CHANGE THE WORLD (Jan. 9, 2012), http://blog.guykawasaki.com/2012/01/how-to-create-an-enchanting-pitch-officeandguyk.html.

"picture is worth a thousand words.") Investors will remember an image more easily than words. Quickly introduce the villain (i.e., the unmet need) and the hero—your product—and share the stage with others in your company. (See Chapter 9 about teams.) After all, investors invest in teams, especially teams made up of individuals they know, have trust in, and that have performed previously. Provide financial information about your projected return on investment for the investor that is confident but realistic. Investors like to invest in founders with confidence, but make sure your projections provide them with realistic goals that can be achieved. Above all, be able to explain what your business does in less than 120 seconds in a way that gives the investor the essence of your company and his or her opportunity for financial reward. I recently had an entrepreneur come to see me. It took her well over an hour to explain her business to me. No investor will spend the time or have the desire to invest in a company whose unmet need cannot be communicated in the time it takes to wait in line in the morning for a cup of coffee.

Structuring Early Investments

Structuring early investment in a startup is often done with convertible loans—a form of investment that will enable the entrepreneur to postpone the valuation of his or her company until the next round of investment.

Essentially, a convertible loan is a hybrid between an equity and debt investment. The investor loans money to the company pursuant to an above interest market rate. Sometimes the investor has a right to convert the loan to equity in connection with the next round of equity, and other times the investor *is required* to convert the loan to equity at the next round of equity. Founders will generally want to require or have the option to require an investor to convert. Investors will want to control this option. It is all a matter of negotiation and leverage among the founders and the investors. Often investors who make convertible loans are given a "sweetener" in connection with the loan in the form of a discount on a subsequent round or penny warrants. For example, if the investor loans $100 to the company, and the next round of investment is priced at $1.00 per share, then he or she may be given the opportunity to convert his or her loan at $.90 per share. This 10 percent discount pays the investor for having faith in the company early in its development and obviates the need to value the company at such an early stage. Penny warrants serve the same purpose. The company issues the investor a warrant, which is a right to purchase a certain number of shares at an agreed upon strike price equal to the then-current value per share or the value to be determined in the next round into which the debt converts. The effect of a warrant guarantees the investor additional shares in the company in exchange for his or her investment. I prefer using the "discount to the next round approach" simply because it avoids the additional paperwork of the warrant. Although when showing convertible loans on an as-diluted basis, do not forget to apply the discount in your calculations.

I had an entrepreneur ask me recently if convertible debt will scare away the next round of investment because it will be listed on the balance sheet as debt. First of all, convertible debt is really a type of equity and so is not usually listed on a balance sheet as straight debt. In addition, investors who are interested in your company will not be scared away because you have taken in early convertible debt investors. Subsequent investors may try to renegotiate the terms of the debt, but if the company is solid the investors will understand why the original investment was made as convertible debt and will look at such investment as early confidence by the debt holders in your company.

Many states have "angel tax credits" to encourage investment in early stage companies. In general, these statutes provide a credit to investors who invest in companies that are located in the state where the credit is issued. The investor does not generally have to be a resident of the state where the company is located. The investor usually receives a credit to his or her state income tax if the investor is a resident of the issuing state, or receives an actual check from the state for the amount of the credit if the investor is not a resident of the state. Entrepreneurs must apply to the state for certification pursuant to the fund. Both equity investments and convertible debt are generally eligible in most states for credit under these statutes. Read the fine print of the statute for the state in which your business is located. Generally there are limited funds available under these statutory rubrics, so entrepreneurs are wise to understand the application process, determine if their companies will fall within any limitations on application (e.g., company must have a technology focus), and apply each year at the very moment when the application process opens. One startup I know of very cleverly required investors to invest the credit they received back into the company. This allowed the company to leverage the money of the investors as well as the credit in a real and tangible way.

The Real World

Sara Russick, co-founder of the angel investment group Gopher Angels, highlighted what she believes are the required elements of a good pitch by a company that is ripe for angel investment:

1. A good, strong team that has the ability to communicate and a strong and evident moral compass that aligns with the investors' world view.
2. Easy to understand message as to how the market for your product or service meets a current and important unmet need and how you will be able to get to market first.
3. A solid growth plan with realistic financials based on achievable assumptions.
4. Know your numbers backward, forwards, and sideways.

According to Sara and Tom Vettel, CEO and managing partner of Atlas Capital Partners, LLC, angels want to receive a 20 to 30 percent interest in a company in exchange for their investment, and possibly a board seat. They consider companies with varying pre-money valuations and will invest varying amounts depending on whether there is a "lead angel" or individuals are investing in the round. The average angel round is in the $600,000 range, but that number can increase if there is a "lead angel." The angel will want some sort of protection to get to the next level of investments, such as preemptive rights, which give then current investors the opportunity to buy into a new round to maintain their percentage ownership. This is why discounts and contractual terms like preemptive rights are so important.

Takeaways from Chapter 8

- *First,* assess the pros and cons of partnering with others who provide financial support.

- *Second,* after deciding to accept investments, do research to select the "right" investor for the company and think through the terms on which investments will be accepted.
- *Third,* communicate in your pitch the following four key elements: (1) a strong management team, (2) the unmet need your product or service addresses, (3) your company's solid growth plan and realistic financials, and (4) know your financials and be able to discuss them thoroughly.
- *Fourth,* always be able to explain the business in two minutes or less.
- *Fifth,* determine how best to structure investments (e.g., convertible loans) to create an attractive investment and to protect the company.
- *Sixth,* seek to capitalize on angel tax credits if granted in your state.

9

Teams, Compensation, and Protection of Information

"Nobody accomplishes success by themselves." - Malcom Gladwell

One of the most important elements of a successful business is the management and employee team an entrepreneur builds. The concepts of a business will change over time. However, the team an entrepreneur identifies and hires to execute on that business concept as it changes, grows, and scales is critical.

As I said in Chapter 8, investors invest in people. They invest in people they trust and with whom they have aligned values and passion. I know of several serial entrepreneurs who did not have success with every single business they started, but who did have the deep confidence of a group of investors who wanted to participate with and invest in them in every new venture. These investors were willing to bet on these entrepreneurs and their abilities to form a team and execute on an idea. They understood not every idea would be a winner and earn them a solid financial return, but had deep trust in the individuals and were willing to take risks because of their demonstrated ability.

Entrepreneurs gain others' trust and firm belief in their reliability, truth, ability, and strength in many ways, including tangible success in prior ventures, demonstration of reliability by accomplishing stated goals, association with the investor for many years so that the investor knows the person and his psyche, and affiliation by the entrepreneur with others in whom the investor trusts.

Developing a Strong Team

Developing a strong team always creates challenges in a startup. The team members are generally required to have trust in the entrepreneur (i.e., the team leader) as well. Entrepreneurs are better off hiring fewer team members with higher quality than more team members who are "B, C or D players." Sometimes, however, when an entrepreneur hires a team member who was an "A" player in another environment in which the entrepreneur worked with the team member, the new hire is not always successful in a new context.

Therefore, the adage "be slow to hire and quick to fire" is very applicable to startup companies. Indeed, business people often refer to the "80/20" rule when dealing with a problematic employee whose performance or even behavior are detrimental to the company or do not meet the expectations of the entrepreneur and the rest of the team. The "80/20" rule means that a company's leadership will spend 80 percent of the time managing the problematic employee and 20 percent of its time managing others. As a result, the entrepreneur's time and energy is drained.

Interviewing Techniques

Consider using a behavioral based approach when interviewing. Such an approach enables you to see how a candidate would react in specific employment-related situations based on how he or she has handled prior situations. Examples of questions an entrepreneur might use in an interview would be:

- *Describe a situation in which you made a sale when you did not think you could.*
- *What do you do when your schedule is interrupted?*
- *Describe a time when you worked under pressure and you had positive results and negative results.*
- *How have you gone above and beyond the call of duty?*
- *Give me an example of a goal you had and how you reached it.*
- *Tell me about a time where you have motivated co-workers.*

- *Tell me about a situation where you had a difficult time with a boss or vendor and how you handled it.*
- *Describe a situation in which you were a good/bad listener.*

The key is that the questions should be open-ended and the answers are used to gain additional information about the potential employee. These sorts of interviews often take an hour or two, but the information you will obtain will be well worth it. Have someone else present with you at the interview to take notes, so that you do not have to worry about writing things down.

Compensation

Properly compensating an employee or contractor in a startup presents a variety of challenges and considerations. Should the compensation be in equity or cash? Should the compensation vest based on time or performance standards? How will the performance of the employee/contractor be measured to determine whether or not he or she will receive the compensation that vests?

Using a combination of types of compensation is often effective, because the company can mitigate the risk it takes with a specific hire. In addition, paying a portion of an employee's compensation in cash limits the amount of equity given to the employee, and as a result is less dilutive of the equity of the company. However, often the only commodity a company has to pay early hires is equity. Therefore, equity that incorporates a balanced combination of time-based incentives and performance-based incentives is effective, because it serves both as "golden handcuffs"—the time element and incentive to grow the company—the performance-based element. For example, an employee can be granted options to purchase one hundred units, twenty-five of which will vest in equal increments on the first, second, and third anniversary of the employee's commencement of employment with the company, if at such anniversary the employee is still then employed by the company. The remaining 75 percent of the options would vest on the first, second, and third anniversary of the employee's commencement of employment with the company if certain milestones are achieved. It is sometimes difficult to set milestones for more than a year at a time. In such a case, the company and the employee can set the milestones for the first year and then agree to set the remaining milestones at the end of each succeeding year. The milestones should be objective—for example, execution of contracts for an aggregate of $_____ in revenue, or succeeding to achieve certification needed from an outside regulatory agency or institution or collections from customers in amounts equal to or exceeding an agreed upon dollar amount. Milestones should not include things like "the employee will use his efforts to bring in more sales" or "the employee will try his best to hire a new sales team." These types of milestones cannot be objectively evaluated. The vesting of equity that is tied to time and/or milestones is effective to keep an employee engaged in the business.

The entrepreneur should also consider the difference between granting options and granting warrants as compensation and the costs and benefits associated with each. Typically warrants do not vest over time. They are granted in exchange for services provided by consultants and other third parties and generally do not have a vesting schedule associated with them. Options are generally issued pursuant to a company option plan that will provide more details about the issuance of the options and also provide a vesting schedule after issuance.

Purchase of equity pursuant to a warrant or an option must have a purchase price designated. This purchase price is often referred to as a "strike price." The strike price for options or warrants usually is at the then current value of the equity into which the options or warrants convert. For example, if a share of common stock is worth $.50 at the time the option is issued, then the "strike price" at which the shares are purchased would be $.50 per share. The type of warrants issued in a non-compensatory manner as a sweetener to outside investors is a different instrument than compensatory options and warrants (see Chapter 8).

Termination

Difficult and awkward challenges are presented when a company needs to end the employment/contractor relationship with an individual. However, if you have an employee or contractor who is not working well in your company, cut your losses quickly and move on. It will certainly be better for your company and in all likelihood better for the person involved. This is a point at which legal counsel should be consulted. You do not want to leave yourself open to possible discrimination claims or lawsuits by a person you terminate.

Independent Contractor or Employee

Entrepreneurs often struggle with whether to engage a person whom they believe will be a good contributor to their company as an independent contractor or employee. There are very specific laws governing whether an individual can be classified as an independent contractor. Because you pay an independent contractor a "gross amount" and do not withhold taxes, this avenue is often attractive to both the entrepreneur and the person he or she wants to hire. However, there are steep penalties for engaging someone as an independent contractor if he or she does not meet the appropriate legal tests for doing so. This is another example of a time it is wise to consult with legal counsel—before you engage the person, not after.

Non-Disclosure Agreements

In addition, it is critical to have the person you intend to engage or hire sign a confidentiality agreement (sometimes called a Non-Disclosure Agreement or NDA for short) that has provisions addressing inventions and nonsolicitation.

Let us deconstruct the critical elements an NDA should contain for an independent contractor or employee.

First, the agreement must contain appropriate language defining what is to be considered confidential. Typical language defining "confidentiality" would be the following:

> CONFIDENTIAL INFORMATION means information developed by [employee/contractor] as a result of the [employee/contractor's] consultation, work or services with, for, on behalf of or in conjunction with the Company and information relating to the Company's processes and

> products, including information relating to research, development, manufacturing, know-how, formulae, product ideas, inventions, trade secrets, patents, patent applications, systems, products, programs and techniques and any secret proprietary or confidential information, knowledge or data of the Company. All information, disclosed to the [employee/contractor], or to which the [employee/contractor] obtains access, whether originated by the [employee/contractor] or by others, which is created by the Company as confidential or which the [employee/contractor] has reasonable basis to believe is confidential, will be presumed to be Confidential Information.

There are generally four exceptions to the definition of "Confidential Information." These include information that (i) the employee/contractor can establish by documentation was known to the employee/contractor prior to receipt from the Company; (ii) is lawfully disclosed to the employee/contractor by a third party not deriving the same from the Company; (iii) is presently in the public domain or becomes a part of the public domain through no fault of the employee/contractor; or (iv) is required by law to be disclosed.

The NDA should also make clear that the employee/contractor must return all confidential information in its possession to the company when his or her affiliation or employment with the company ends.

The NDA for an employee/contractor should also contain a section on inventions that makes clear that discoveries during the employee/contractor's association with the company belong to the company. A common definition of "Inventions" would be:

"Inventions" mean discoveries, improvements, inventions, ideas, and works of authorship (whether or not patentable or copyrightable) conceived or made by the [employee/contractor], either solely or jointly with others, relating to any consultation, work or services performed by the [employee/contractor] with, for, on behalf of or in conjunction with the company or based on or derived from Confidential Information.

The NDA itself provides that the contractor/employee cannot use confidential information except in connection with his or her work for the company. In addition, the inventions section should make clear that inventions developed during the time the employee/contractor works for the company that relate in any way to the company (whether or not the invention is developed on particular days on which the employee/contractor is working for the company) are the sole and exclusive property of the company. It is also important that the NDA specify that all such rights the employee/contractor has in such inventions are automatically assigned by the employee/contractor to the company.

Sometimes a potential employee/contractor will want the company to make an exception for certain personal inventions the employee/contractor has developed. The best way to do this is to list the inventions on a separate attachment to the agreement and make clear they are not subject to the agreement.

The final section of this sort of agreement with an employee/contractor will typically prevent the employee/contractor from leaving the company and taking employees with him or her, interfering with current relationships with customers and suppliers, and soliciting customers.

Drafts of these sorts of agreements must be provided to the employee/contractor prior to the time he or she becomes employed by or engaged by the company and must be signed prior to the time such person begins working for the agreement to be enforceable. By not providing a draft in advance and having the agreement signed before the individual begins working, the company risks that the individual will leave and take employees and important relationships with suppliers and customers, and the company will have no recourse to the employee for such action.

Takeaways from Chapter 9

- *First*, understand that when investors invest in a startup company they are investing in people, so focus on building a management team investors will trust and into which they will want to invest.

- *Second*, strive to achieve tangible success in numerous ventures, accomplish stated goals, and associate with investors for many years to develop a mutual personal and professional understanding to demonstrate the entrepreneur's trustworthiness to investors.

- *Third*, keep in mind the adage "be slow to hire and quick to fire" to develop a strong management team that does not drain the resources of the company and the entrepreneur.

- *Fourth*, consider using a behavioral interview process when hiring employees to best determine how each candidate would react in specific employment related situations based on how he or she has handled other experiences.

- *Fifth*, consider combining different forms of employee compensation, such as cash and equity that vest based on different criteria, to minimize dilution of company equity but still incentivize strong performance and longevity with the company.

- *Sixth*, ensure that every employee or contractor executes a confidentiality agreement to protect the confidential information, inventions, and intellectual property of the company.

- *Seventh*, ensure that every employee or contractor executes a noncompetition and non-solicitation agreement to prevent a disgruntled employee or contractor from leaving the company and attempting to take the company's talent or important relationships with suppliers and customers.

10

Governance

*"The most difficult thing is the decision to act,
the rest is merely tenacity." - Amelia Earhart*

Governance is the control or influence a group of people have on those who operate a startup. Some governance systems make decisions that directly affect the founders and the company, often referred to as a "fiduciary board." Other types of governance systems only advise the CEO and leave the actual decision making to the CEO, and are called an "advisory board."

Types of Boards

The three factors that typically influence how a company is governed are size, ownership, and maturity of the entity. Initially, during the time a company has no outside investors, there is also no formal board of directors and the company's decisions are usually made informally by the founders pursuant to discussion and consensus. The tipping point for a company to organize a formal board of directors is generally its first formal outside round of investment. Often, investors who purchase equity in the company's first real outside round will insist on a board seat as part of the investment package. This first "real" group generally includes angel investors.

Advisory Board

The main difference between a board of advisors and a fiduciary board is their power, control, and duties. An advisory board can provide the CEO in an early stage company with help, connections, and ideas. Often the scheduling of advisory board meetings provides the CEO and his or her team with the discipline to develop periodic reports. Knowing that a meeting will be held forces the CEO and his or her team to think about the meeting agenda, review the financials, and determine what to present to the board. This discipline will be well served once the company needs to organize a more formal fiduciary board.

I have seen advisory boards that meet as often as once a month and as infrequently as twice a year. The purpose of an advisory board should be to challenge the assumptions and milestones created by the CEO and his or her team as the business is developing. The advisory board can be composed of persons who are knowledgeable in the startup's industry, or persons who are knowledgeable about delivery of a product in another industry with application to this industry. For example, the holding company of the online school Capella University asked Howard Schultz to serve on its board several years ago. I believe Capella did this not because it wanted to start selling coffee, but rather because it wanted to develop an international distribution network and likely believed Mr. Schultz's experience in this area would be helpful. Therefore, it is always important when developing an advisory board to look broadly at the needs of the company. I recommend that the CEO complete the matrix in Exhibit 10-1 as a means to identify those skills he or she believes will be helpful and necessary to be represented on its first advisory board. It is wise to not fill the board with a number of "yes people" but with smart, inquisitive, experienced advisors who will challenge the assumptions, milestones, and metrics of the business and provide valuable advice.

Board Matrix Worksheet	# of Current Members	# of Prospective Members	Total Members
Areas of Expertise/Leadership Qualities			
Administration/Management			0
Early-stage organizations/start-ups			0
Financial oversight			0
Fundraising			0
Government			0
Investment management			0
Law			0
Leadership skills/motivator			
Marketing, public relations			0
Human resources			0
Strategic planning			0
Physical plant (architect, engineer)			0
Real estate			0
Understanding of community needs			0
Technology			0
Other			0

Resources			
Money to give			0
Access to money			0
Access to other resources (foundations, corporate support)			0
Availability for active participation (solicitation visits, grant writing)			0

Community Connections			
Religious organizations			0
Corporate			0
Education			0
Media			0
Political			0
Philanthropy			0
Small business			0
Social services			0
Other			0

Personal Style			
Consensus builder			0
Good communicator			0
Strategist			0
Team member			
Visionary			0

Age			
Under 18			0
19 – 34			0
35 – 50			0
51 – 65			0
Over 65			0

Gender			
Male			0
Female			0

Race/Ethnicity			
African American/Black			0
Asian/Pacific Islander			0
Caucasian			0
Hispanic/Latino			0
Native American/Indian			0
Other			0

Excerpted from The Board Building Cycle: Nine Steps to Finding, Recruiting, and Engaging Nonprofit Board Members, Second Edition, by Berit M. Lakey. BoardSource, 2007.

It is important that one member of the advisory board be tasked with taking minutes, keeping attendance, and developing a periodic agenda. This helps the board meetings run more efficiently and provide the best advice to the company's CEO. This task could rotate among the board members at the meetings, or you could appoint one person to be the chair of the advisory board. The chair will be the person who should be asking for the agenda ten days prior to the meeting, keep the meeting running efficiently, and take and circulate notes. Advisory board members are generally given options to purchase equity in the company in exchange for service on the advisory board in an amount equal to .25 percent to .50 percent of the company when issued. Generally, the chair of the advisory board will receive additional payment for agreeing to perform the tasks required of the Chairman. One advisory board that I worked with only granted options if the advisory board member attended the meeting in person.

Fiduciary Board

A fiduciary board is a board that serves to protect the management of the company from taking actions that are contrary to the interests of the shareholders. Generally, the CEO of a company reports to the board of directors which gives the board the ability to fire, change the salary of or otherwise make changes in the functions performed by the CEO. The reason for this chain of command is to provide a system of checks and balances so that the CEO cannot act in a way that is detrimental to the company and the interests of all shareholders.

Often the first CEO of a company is the founder. In addition, the investments by the first set of outside investors generally give them only a minority interest in the company. As a result, the first formal board provides balance to the needs and desires of the founder who in most instances continues to own a majority of the company and provides protection to the new shareholders of the company.

The first formal board of directors of a startup is often actually organized simultaneously with the closing of the first formal angel investment in a company. Some angels will insist that if they are going to invest in the company they must also be given a seat on the company's board. This bird's eye view by an angel of the operation of the company gives the angel the opportunity to make sure its money is being put to good use.

The composition of the first formal fiduciary board generally gives a seat to the founder or co-founders, one or two investors, and an independent board member. The independent board member generally has industry experience or other complementary experience useful for the startup and is chosen by the other board members.

Boards of directors with fiduciary duties should be composed of odd numbers of people. Otherwise, decisions can be hamstrung by failure of the board to agree. The main jobs of a fiduciary board are the following: hiring and firing the CEO, approving annual budgets, additional fundraising, capital expenditures, and advising about strategy.

Election of a Fiduciary Board

There is often confusion about how a fiduciary board is elected. The governing documents of the company (for a corporation, articles of incorporation, bylaws, and a shareholders' agreement; and for a limited liability company, a member control agreement, LLC agreement or operating agreement) will provide how the board is selected. Typically upon the first investment by a group of angels, the governing documents are revised to provide that certain groups of shareholders (or members in an LLC) have the rights to elect a fixed number of directors.

For example, the governing documents might provide something like the following: "The board of directors of the Company shall consist of five directors. [names of two company founders] shall each have the right to designate a board member. The owners of the investment closed on _____, 20__ shall have the right to designate one board member. One board member will be a holder of common stock in the company, shall not be one of the founders or an investor in the investment closed on _____, 20__ and shall be elected by all common equity holders. The fifth board member shall be elected by all remaining board members, shall be an independent board member and shall not be an equity investor in the Company."

In the foregoing example, the board would then consist of the two company founders' designees and each can designate him or herself, one person designated by the angel investors, one person designated by all equity investors, and one person agreed upon by the other board members. This gives the board five members, only one of whom holds no company equity, all of whom have disparate interests in the company, and can provide lively discussion and good real-time advice.

I often recommend that one person be designated chair of the board. The founders almost always want to be the chair of the board. My advice would be to elect another party as the chair so that the founder has a natural ally who can help shape board meetings and discussions among board members. Again, the chair is typically provided with additional compensation.

The board also needs to identify a compensation committee at this stage. This committee typically does not include the founders and does include the independent director. This is the committee who either reviews the compensation recommendations for the CEO and option grants for other employees and either votes on them independently or makes a recommendation to the full board for approval.

Any time the CEO has an important issue to bring to a board member, he or she is well served by talking with the opinion leaders on the board, and perhaps all board members prior to the meeting. I call this "the meeting before the meeting." Board members should not learn of important issues for the first time at a board meeting. The CEO, by talking with board members individually, can gage how the board will react to an important new issue and plan accordingly.

Fiduciary Duties

Fiduciary duty owed by a board member to a company and its shareholders or members is composed of two elements. These two elements are referred to as the "duty of loyalty" and the "duty of care." These elements are *not* required of advisory board members.

The "duty of loyalty" requires each board member to make decisions in "good faith" and to act in a way that does not cause the director personal economic conflict. The definition of "good faith" means the board member cannot make decisions that favor his or her own self-interest over that of the company and would also prohibit the board member from taking corporate opportunities for his or her own benefit. This second prohibition on taking corporate opportunities for his or her own benefit is often referred to in legal jargon as "usurpation of corporate opportunity." Simply, the duty of loyalty is designed to prohibit a board member from letting his or her personal business interests influence his or her decisions on behalf of the company.

The second element of fiduciary duty that is imposed on a director of a board is called the "duty of care." The duty of care requires a board member to make informed decisions using all available information. This duty has been defined by case laws over the years as requiring directors to demand that all available information to make a decision be provided in sufficient time prior to the time a decision is made to enable detailed review, hiring board experts if necessary and understanding how the action presented for vote will affect the company, its finances, and its goals and objectives. It is for this reason that the founders are well advised to provide board packets to the board members at least a week in advance. These packets should include financial reports (including an analysis of budget to actual income statement), sales reports, and an agenda. It is sometimes very difficult for a startup to provide a board packet a week in advance, but it helps management develop discipline and will make the board meetings more efficient and worthwhile for all involved.

Founders should never design an agenda so that subjects on which they seek input from board members, such as growth options and new financing, are to be discussed at the end of the board meeting. These are the topics where your board can provide tremendous value. I have seen far too many board agendas place these issues at the end of meeting agendas, where there is little time to discuss. The result is that board members are frustrated hearing reports on matters they could have read in advance and then do not have sufficient time to provide appropriate guidance and strategic advice to management.

Indemnification of Directors of Fiduciary Boards

Companies often are required by state statute to indemnify board members for claims made against them in their capacity as board members. This means that if a third party brings a lawsuit against the company and its individual directors, the company is required to pay for the fees the directors incur in connection with such lawsuit. Sometimes these sorts of liabilities can be mitigated by a company having "directors and officers" insurance, often referred to as "D&O" insurance. These policies are often costly and unfortunately many companies do not seek proper counsel when first purchasing D&O insurance, only to find out later that the policy is adequate to reimburse them for legal expenses and the costs of claims. When it comes to insurance policies, the answer is really in the "fine print." It is important to find a well-versed insurance lawyer who can read and understand the fine print and advise the company whether or not the policy that it is being offered is sufficient for its needs.

The Real World

Kaye O'Leary, who has served as CFO for many companies including Bucca and Caribou Coffee and is now a consultant who assists companies with governance related matters, explains that the makeup of boards vary with the size of the business. A person who might make an excellent board member of a public company is not necessarily the right person to serve on the board of a startup. The challenges and opportunities in a startup vary greatly from those in a publicly held company. Kaye advises that companies pick board members carefully and make sure they have the appropriate experience to provide value to the board on which they are asked to serve.

It is important to choose all board members carefully. As Kaye counseled, "like Caesar's wife, board members must be above suspicion." Choose board members wisely, make sure their world view is aligned with yours, and make sure they have the time to devote to being an active and involved board member.

Takeaways from Chapter 10

- *First*, consider the three factors that typically influence how a company is governed: size, ownership (and whether the company has accepted outside investments), and maturity of the company to make the decision as to how the company should be governed and when to establish a formal board of directors.
- *Second*, understand the costs and benefits of and differences between advisory boards of directors and fiduciary boards of directors to decide what type of board is appropriate for the company.
- *Third*, realize that often angel investors will insist on a board seat as a condition to its investment to maximize the company's chances at obtaining angel investments.

- *Fourth*, when creating a fiduciary board, choose an odd number of board members and select an independent board member to prevent deadlocks and provide industry expertise or other complementary knowledge and experience.

- *Fifth*, when creating a fiduciary board, consider electing someone to be the chair of the board who is a natural ally with the founder and who can shape board meetings and discussions.

- *Sixth*, when creating a fiduciary board, establish a compensation committee comprised of at least one independent director to review the compensation structure of the company and provide unbiased recommendations to the board of directors regarding compensation.

- *Seventh*, understand that the two fiduciary duties imposed by law on a fiduciary board are the duty of loyalty and the duty of care and what is required by each of these duties to protect the interests of the company and avoid legal liability on the part of the board.

- *Eighth*, avoid scheduling important discussion topics at the end of board meetings to ensure time does not run out, causing the company to lose the opportunity to receive the advice and insight of board members.

- *Ninth*, remember that state statutes often require the company to indemnify board members for claims made against them in their capacity as board members and consider obtaining officer and director insurance to mitigate the risks of incurring costs as a result of third party lawsuits brought against individual directors or officers.

11

Prescription for Legal Intervention

"The meeting of two personalities is like the contact of two chemical substances: if there is any reaction, both are transformed." - Carl Jung

This book is designed to help entrepreneurs better understand the process that goes into developing successful startups and become smart consumers of legal services. This last chapter is devoted to specifically identifying those situations where an entrepreneur is best served by seeking legal advice.

Choosing the Type of Entity

This book in Chapter 4 provides information regarding the types of entities entrepreneurs can use to organize a startup. There are specific reasons an entrepreneur would select a C corp, an S corp or a limited liability company.

The entrepreneur should first develop a list of goals it wants to achieve by its structure. This list might include the following goals:

1. Need pass-through entity for tax purposes;
2. Want to make sure that all types of investors can invest, including entities and individuals;
3. Do not want double level of taxation;
4. Plan to seek investment from coasts; or
5. Want founders to be employees and not have to receive all payments as distributions.

Counsel can then help the entrepreneur determine the type of entity that will best suit his or her needs.

Choosing Where to Incorporate or Organize

Chapter 4 of this book also discusses the advantages and disadvantages of organizing in various states. Where an entity will organize is also a valuable topic to discuss with counsel. The goals for where to organize might include the following:

1. Want state of organization with well-developed business doctrines;
2. Initially plan to do business in home state only and do not plan to have offices in other states;
3. Plan to seek investors from throughout the United States;
4. Will do most of business in a state with no state income tax; or
5. Want ability to take advantage of investor credit available in a particular state.

Naming of Company and Naming of Brand

The name of a company and the name of a brand to be used to sell a company's products or services are two completely different elements. The name of the company is used to identify it for purposes of state organization, authorization to do business, and taxing purposes. The name of a brand used to describe either a product or service may be the same as the name of the company or may be different.

Name of Company

The name of the company is registered with the secretary of state of the state in which the entity is organized. This same name is also registered with other states in which the company needs to qualify to do business and/or pay taxes. If the name of the company is already used in a second state, the company will need to apply for a "d/b/a" in the second state since the secretary of state of the second state will not allow two entities to be registered with the same name. An entrepreneur can find the website of the secretary of state in which he or she decides to organize and check the name availability. Such a check is wise prior to deciding on the name. If the company is certain it will do business in a second state, it is wise to check the website of the secretary of state for the second state to make sure the same name is available.

Name of Brand

Deciding what to use as a trademark for a brand is a separate issue. Once a brand name is determined, an entrepreneur should check the website of the Patent and Trademark Office[26] and search for the brand name in the category in which it will be used. If the name is already taken, it is wise to develop a new name for the brand. If the brand name is not used, it is wise to consult counsel that has access to more sophisticated databases to see if the name is available to trademark. Before you start developing and using the brand, it is important to make sure it is a name that can be ultimately protected.

Domain Names

Domain names are a third category of names and can be easily secured by an entrepreneur through an Internet search. Choose a domain name that is easily identifiable with your brand and reserve under as many top level domain names as possible.

Filing Initial Organization Documents

Once you have determined what type of entity you should organize, what state you should organize in, and the name of your company, an entrepreneur can generally do the initial filing by him or herself. The website of the secretary of state of the state in which you organize should have a simple form for the kind of organization you want to form. This can be completed and filed by the entrepreneur.

After the initial filing of the organizational documents, an entrepreneur should consult counsel to seek assistance in developing initial minutes, a buy/sell agreement, and bylaws or other governing documents.

---

[26] *The United States Patent and Trademark Office*, USPTO.GOV, www.uspto.gov.

Financing Documents and Options/Warrants

It is wise for entrepreneurs to consult counsel when others are ready to invest in the startup. Again, it is key to identify the goals of the investment and seek help from counsel to structure the investment accordingly. The goals for initial investment can include:

1. Need cash to develop initial concept.
2. Want to dilute founders as little as possible.
3. Would like to take cash on as-needed basis or would like to take cash to cover needs for specific period of time.
4. Want to reward those who invest early with right to invest in later rounds.
5. Option plans, option forms, and warrant forms should be developed by counsel.

Other Situations

An entrepreneur is well served after the foregoing matters are established to keep in regular touch with its counsel. Periodic lunches should be scheduled so that the entrepreneur can update counsel on the current situation of the company. In addition, many counsel will attend board meetings of a startup without charge. This enables advice to be given in "real time" and missteps to be minimized.

Choosing a Business Lawyer

Choosing a business lawyer has as much to do with chemistry as anything else. Find counsel who is experienced in working with startups and has the capacity to grow with your business. Think about the following matters when finding the right counsel:

1. How much experience does he or she have working with startups?
2. Does the lawyer have expertise in or have colleagues who specialize in employment, intellectual property, commercial contract negotiations, or litigation?
3. What types of early stage financing has the lawyer done during the years?

4. What will be the fee structure?
5. Will the lawyer you interview be the counsel you work with after you hire him or her?
6. Do you like the lawyer you interviewed?
7. Does the lawyer have connections in the startup community?

Counsel for your startup is an integral part of your team. Choose this team member carefully.

12

Frequently Asked Questions

Q: How should I come up with an idea for a startup that will be successful?

A: Identify an unmet need and find a way to fill that need. Have passion for your idea and a deep sense of focus. Rather than being a perfectionist, strive to develop a product or service where all parties involved benefit.

Q: Do I really need a business plan?

A: The process of developing a business plan is more important than the end-product. You need to constantly evaluate your business idea and be open to changing it as you obtain new facts and ideas. Modify your business plan as your ideas change. Balance carefully the time you spend planning and the time you spend implementing your plan.

Q: How do I develop projections for a new company?

A: To develop projections for a startup you need to make assumptions regarding the progress of your business. After you do research, you make an educated guess about the progress you think your business can make. Then determine how much money you need to accomplish each of your projections. Projections are simply the quantification of your business plan.

Q: **How do I know what kind of structure I should use for my company and in what state I should organize?**

A: Consult an attorney regarding the best type of structure and in what state to organize. There are many factors that will influence the decision and an attorney who works with startups will be able to guide you in this important decision.

Q: Some of my friends have advised me to split equity with business partners when we start the business and others have suggested I wait until after the business appears to be successful. Is there a right answer to this question?

A: There is definitely a difference of opinion among experts about when is the right time to divide up the equity in the business. To split equity you need to have honest and transparent discussions with your business partners. The advantage to waiting until later to split equity is that you will know more about the contributions each of you will make. The advantage to splitting equity early is that it may be easier to have an open and honest discussion before the business gets started.

Q: **How are startups valued?**

A: There is no universal methodology to value a startup. Valuation is determined by negotiation between an investor and a founder. The percentage of the company the investor seeks to obtain in exchange for his or her investment determines the value of the company.

Q: **What does pre-money and post-money mean?**

A: Pre-money and post-money are terms used in valuation discussions. The pre-money value of a company is the value you and your investor agree upon prior to his or her investment. The post-money value of a company is the pre-money value of the company plus the investment made by your new investor. For example, if the pre-money value of a company is $2,000,000 and your investor invests $1,000,000, then the post-money value of a company is $3,000,000. The investor then owns 1/3 of the company, i.e., $1,000,000/$3,000,000.

Q: Should I take outside investors into my company?

A: If you take outside investors into your company be prepared that you now have additional partners. Some investors are passive and others are very active and will want to be involved in your business. Carefully interview investors to make sure their interest and commitment to your company matches your worldview.

Q: Are elevator speeches and pitches really important when building a startup?

A: It is critical that you be able to describe your startup with very few words. The more succinct you can be in describing your startup the easier it will be to catch the attention of potential customers and investors.

Q: How important is the team I develop in my startup?

A: Investors invest in people, not ideas. Therefore, the team you organize to develop your startup is very important. Investors will be looking for the collective experience your team has in creating successful companies and executing on new ideas.

Q: What is the difference between an advisory board and a board of directors?

A: An advisory board is a group of people who provide you with guidance but have no right to vote on matters regarding your company. A board of directors has a fiduciary duty to other stockholders in the company and does have a right to vote on matters regarding your company. A board of directors (sometimes called a fiduciary board) has the right to fire the CEO. Therefore, choose carefully who will constitute your board of directors. Unless investors insist there be a fiduciary board, I always recommend that a startup begin with an advisory board only.

Q: What are the most important things I should consult a lawyer about in the early phases of my startup?

A: • Choosing the type of entity
        • Choosing the state where you will organize
        • Naming the company
        • Naming and protecting your brand
        • Taking investments in your company and dividing equity
        • Issuing options and warrants

ABOUT THE AUTHOR

Terri Krivosha, a partner with the law firm of Maslon Edelman Borman & Brand LLP, is passionate about helping businesses grow, succeed, and scale. She works with a strong network of entrepreneurial and dynamic businesses and their funders, advising them on all matters as they grow their businesses. She served as chair of her firm for four years, and this experience running a business has enabled her to understand and empathize with her clients' needs and challenges.

ASPATORE